Intro to Joy

Intro to Joy

Heather Jean Wilson Torosyan

Community Christian Ministries
P.O. Box 9754, Moscow, Idaho 83843
208.883.0997 | www.ccmbooks.org

Heather Jean Wilson Torosyan, *Intro to Joy*

ISBN: 978-1-882840-42-7

Cover design by Samuel Dickison.
Interior design by Valerie Anne Bost.
Printed in the United States of America.

21 22 23 24 25 26 27 28 29 30 9 8 7 6 5 4 3 2 1

To God, my exceeding joy.

CONTENTS

SECTION ONE

God and Joy

SECTION TWO

Our Joy in the Lord

SECTION THREE

Rejoicing in Salvation

SECTION FOUR

Rejoice in the Lord & King

SECTION FIVE

Everlasting Joy

SECTION SIX

Complete Joy, Great Joy, and Full Joy

SECTION SEVEN

Temporary Joy

SECTION EIGHT

Joy in His Word and Works

SECTION NINE

Joy in the Gospel

SECTION TEN

Joy in Service and Suffering

SECTION ELEVEN

Rejoicing for Things

FOREWORD

It is a great joy for me to see the completion of this book that contains my beloved wife Heather Jean's years of work on a topic that was very close to her heart.

There is no better way to describe Heather than by her *overflowing* joy in the Lord and her love for the lost. When I first met her, it was this overflowing joy that led me to the Gospel, which brought me into His kingdom, out of darkness.

I encourage you take time to meditate and pray each day on what you read, so that you may also be filled with His *inexpressible, overflowing joy*.

ARARAT TOROSYAN
April 2021

INTRODUCTION

In the past several years, while reading the Scriptures, I started to take note (literally) of verses that blessed me. I began to see different themes in the verses noted. One of those themes was *joy*.

I decided to take all the references to *joy*, *joyful*, and *rejoicing* in the verses I had noted to see what I could find. It was amazing, as Scripture is wont to be. There were the expected themes like singing for joy and joy as the fruit of the Spirit; but there was so much more. So the categorizing began.

In this book, I have written out my thoughts on the different aspects of joy and how this joy can affect us as followers of the Lord Jesus Christ. This is not intended to be an academic treatise, but something that people can read and be encouraged by. There are so many reasons and ways and kinds of joy that it will be hard to not be encouraged.

References are from the New American Standard Bible, so on occasion other translations will read a bit differently. Do not let that worry you; there is so much joy in reading His word that it is better not to get tripped up on little things.

Heather Torosyan
2017

SECTION ONE

God and Joy

DAY

1

Our Exceeding Joy

Vindicate me, O God, and plead my case against an ungodly nation;
O deliver me from the deceitful and unjust man!
For You are the God of my strength; why have You rejected me?
Why do I go mourning because of the oppression of the enemy?

O send out Your light and Your truth, let them lead me;
Let them bring me to Your holy hill
And to Your dwelling places.
Then I will go to the altar of God,
To God my exceeding joy;
And upon the lyre I shall praise You, O God, my God.

Why are you in despair, O my soul?
And why are you disturbed within me?
Hope in God, for I shall again praise Him,
The help of my countenance and my God.
(Psalm 43)

This psalm pleads with God for deliverance. David explains to God that He is the source of his strength, and he wants to know why God has rejected him. He is mourning because he is being oppressed by his enemy. Then he turns to God and prays; he pleas to be led by His light and truth, to return to His holy hill.

When David returns to God's holy hill, he will be able to go to the altar of God, and not just to the altar but also to God Himself, the God whom David recognizes as not only his joy but as his *exceeding* joy.

The outcome of this will be praise to God for being delivered, but also praise to God, his exceeding joy.

David expresses so much joy here, even though it is from a place of feeling desperate. David knows where to look for help. In the final verse, he speaks to his soul asking it why it is in despair, why it is disturbed. He points himself to God, and he knows that he will once again praise Him.

Can we look to God in our troubles and trials and confidently say that He is our exceeding joy? We might have a hard time saying that God is our exceeding joy in normal circumstances, much less during trials. Let us, with David, come to Him and recognize that only He should hold that place in our hearts.

DAY
2

Abide in Him

Just as the Father has loved Me, I have also loved you; abide in My love. If you keep My commandments, you will abide in My love; just as I have kept My Father's commandments and abide in His love. These things I have spoken to you so that My joy may be in you, and *that your joy may be made full.* (John 15:9–11)

In John 14–17 are our Lord's final teachings to His disciples and His prayers for them. In 15:1–11, He speaks to them about abiding in Him. To abide means *to live in.* Jesus is the vine, and we must abide in Him if we are to bear fruit. A branch that is not completely connected to the vine will not produce anything. The juices are just not flowing. In verse 8, Jesus says that the Father is glorified by our bearing of fruit, showing that we are His disciples.

In verses 9–10, Jesus speaks of how the Father has loved Him, and He tells the disciples that in the same way Jesus Himself has loved them. Then He tells them to abide in that love. Next, He explains how we abide in His love: by keeping His commandments. Jesus had kept His Father's commandments and had abided in the Father's love. Keeping God's commandments equals abiding in His love.

So why was Jesus talking about all this abiding and obeying business? "These things I have spoken to you so that My joy may be in you, and that your joy may be made full." The reason Jesus is talking about obeying and abiding is so that His joy may be our joy and that joy would be full.

Abiding in Jesus' love by obeying His commandments will result in His joy being in us. How much joy? Not a little bit of joy. He says that this is all so our joy may be made *full*. Think about a full tank of gas. Our joy tank will be full! That's what Jesus is interested in. There have probably been times in your life when you could say that your joy was full. Jesus is interested in this being *your normal state of affairs*.

Once again, how will this happen? By abiding in Him, which means obeying Him. If you look back at verse 8, you will see that the Father is glorified by this.

Joy does not come through trying to be joyful; it comes when we obey God.

DAY 3

God's Joy over Us

They shall be My people, and I will be their God; and I will give them one heart and one way, that they may fear Me always, for their own good and for the good of their children after them. I will make an everlasting covenant with them that I will not turn away from them, to do them good; and I will put the fear of Me in their hearts so that they will not turn away from Me. *I will rejoice over them to do them good* and will faithfully plant them in this land with all My heart and with all My soul. (Jer. 32:38–41)

Jeremiah 32 begins with Jeremiah being imprisoned, whereupon he buys a field according to God's direction. The LORD proceeds to tell him that the Chaldeans (the Babylonians) are going to come, Jerusalem will be given over to them, and they will set the city on fire (v. 29). The LORD is promising this because Israel had been grossly disobedient, to the point of giving their children as burnt sacrifices to the god Molech (v. 35).

But then God gives hope of a future return to Jerusalem. That will be a time when they will be His people, and He will be their God (v. 38). This return will be based on their having one heart given them by God. There will be an everlasting covenant, because God will put the fear of Himself into their hearts so that they will not turn away from Him as they had done so many times before (vv. 39–40). The fear of the Lord seems to be an integral part of the subsequent joy. Our hearts need to have such a fear that we will not turn away from Him as had happened (and happens) so often.

Then God says that He will rejoice over them! He will "do them good and will faithfully plant them in the land with all [His] heart and with all [His] soul" (v. 41).

God rejoices over them because of what *He* is doing for them, not because of how wonderful they are. Blessing us apparently causes God to rejoice.

I believe it is safe to say that God desires to bless us and rejoice over us. This is a result of our fearing Him and remaining true to Him and not turning away.

DAY

4

The God Who Brings Joy

"Behold, I will bring to [Jerusalem] health and healing, and I will heal them; and I will reveal to them an abundance of peace and truth. I will restore the fortunes of Judah and the fortunes of Israel and will rebuild them as they were at first. I will cleanse them from all their iniquity by which they have sinned against Me, and I will pardon all their iniquities by which they have sinned against Me and by which they have transgressed against Me. *It will be to Me a name of joy, praise and glory before all the nations of the earth* which will hear of all the good that I do for them, and they will fear and tremble because of all the good and all the peace that I make for it." Thus says the Lord, "Yet again there will be heard in this place, of which you say, 'It is a waste, without man and without beast,' . . . *the voice of joy and the voice of gladness*, the voice of the bridegroom and the voice of the bride, the voice of those who say, 'Give thanks to the Lord of hosts, for the Lord is good, for His lovingkindness is everlasting'; and of those who bring a thank offering into the house of the

Lord. For I will restore the fortunes of the land as they were at first," says the Lord. (Jer. 33:6–11)

God's promise of restoration continues in Jeremiah 33. Even though everything in Jerusalem will be broken down and taken over by the Chaldeans due to His people's wickedness, God will yet bring health and healing, and there will be an abundance of peace and truth. The fortunes of Judah and Israel will be restored (vv. 6–7). Their iniquities will be pardoned (v. 8). Then God will rejoice in Jerusalem, a city of forgiven, prospering people.

All the nations of the earth will hear of the good brought about by this great restoration, an abundance of peace, truth, and much healing, with fortunes restored. First, it will be to God a "name of joy, praise, and glory" before those very nations (v. 9). These nations will see God's joy over the city and fear and tremble because of all the good and all the peace that He will make for Jerusalem (v. 9).

God shows His restorative powers here: Jerusalem, which was "a waste, without man or beast" (v. 10), will be a place where the voice of joy and gladness will be heard. Life will be full with all the activities of a healthy society (the voice of the bridegroom and bride), but with a new bond with God. Their joy will be intricately connected to their thanks towards the Lord of hosts for His everlasting lovingkindness (v.11).

I believe that, as redeemed sinners who have received an abundance of peace and truth, we are first *a joy to God* because He has pardoned and cleansed us from our sin. There is no real joy for anyone without this forgiveness. Secondly, our joy will cause those around us to recognize God as *the God who brings joy*, praise, and glory. But our joy, joy in our normal living, should be connected to and accompanied by our thanks to the good LORD for His everlasting lovingkindness (mercy). This is not, nor should it be, a one-time thanks. His mercies are new every morning (Lam. 3:22–23). Let us thank Him for it.

DAY

5

Joy in Finding the Lost

The Lost Sheep

So He told them this parable, saying, "What man among you, if he has a hundred sheep and has lost one of them, does not leave the ninety-nine in the open pasture and go after the one which is lost until he finds it? When he has found it, he lays it on his shoulders, rejoicing. And when he comes home, he calls together his friends and his neighbors, saying to them, *'Rejoice with me, for I have found my sheep which was lost!'* I tell you that in the same way, there will be *more joy in heaven* over one sinner who repents than over ninety-nine righteous persons who need no repentance." (Luke 15:1–10)

The Lost Coin

Or what woman, if she has ten silver coins and loses one coin, does not light a lamp and sweep the house and search carefully until she finds it? When she has found it, she calls together her friends and neighbors, saying, *"Rejoice with me,* for I have found the coin which I had lost!" In the same way, I tell you, *there is joy in the presence of the angels of God over one sinner who repents.* (Luke 15:20–24)

The Lost Son

So he got up and came to his father. But while he was still a long way off, his father saw him and felt compassion for him, and ran and embraced him and kissed him. And the son said to him, "Father, I have sinned against heaven and in your sight; I am no longer worthy to be called your son." But the father said to his slaves, "Quickly bring out the best robe and put it on him, and put a ring on his hand and sandals on his feet; and bring the fattened calf, kill it, and let us eat and celebrate; for this son of mine was dead and has come to life again; he was lost and has been found." And they began to celebrate . . . And he said to him, "Son, you have always been with me, and all that is mine is yours. But we had to celebrate and rejoice, for this brother of yours was dead and has begun to live, and was lost and has been found." (Luke 15:31–32)

These three parables describe how valuable a single person is to the Lord. The lost sheep is searched for by its owner; the lost coin is likewise; and the prodigal son is watched for eagerly by his father. The owners of the lost sheep and lost coin represent our Father in Heaven, as does the father of the lost son.

Notice what the passage says about the owner of the sheep: "When he has found it, he lays it on his shoulders, *rejoicing*. And when he comes home, he calls together his friends and his neighbors saying to them, '*Rejoice with me*.'" The woman looking for her lost coin calls her friends and neighbors. "*Rejoice with me*, for I have found the coin which I had lost!" And the father of the prodigal throws a party. When the brother objects, the father says, "But *we had to celebrate and rejoice*, for this brother of yours was dead and has begun to live, and was lost and has been found."

Jesus says, "I tell you that in the same way, there will be more joy in heaven over one sinner who repents than over ninety-nine righteous persons who need no repentance." *Heaven rejoices when a sinner repents.* In the last parable, the father throws a party, saying that it is only right to rejoice for the return of the prodigal. So not only is heaven rejoicing, but the heavenly Father is rejoicing. It is not only the angels that rejoice over a repentant sinner. *God the Father Himself rejoices* over a lost one being found.

Think about it: God rejoices over each new believer. In Jeremiah 32:41, God says He will rejoice over them to do them good. *God rejoices to do us good.* He rejoices to save us by His grace. He rejoices when the lost are found.

DAY
6

God's Joy in Our Salvation

What do you think? If any man has a hundred sheep, and one of them has gone astray, does he not leave the ninety-nine on the mountains and go and search for the one that is straying? If it turns out that he finds it, truly I say to you, he rejoices over it more than over the ninety-nine that have not gone astray. So it is not the will of your Father who is in heaven that one of these little ones perish. (Matt. 18:12–14)

This is like the previous passage where the shepherd rejoices in finding his sheep. Our God rejoices when one of His sheep is saved and brought into the fold. He does not will that even one of these sheep should perish.

DAY
7

Entering into God's Joy

His master said to him, "Well done, good and faithful slave. You were faithful with a few things, I will put you in charge of many things; *enter into the joy of your master.*" (Matt. 25:21, repeated in v. 23)

This parable shows us the importance of being faithful with what we have been given by God (everything, not just money). When we are faithful, God commends us. The result of that "well done" is entering into the joy of our Master. The Master has a joy that we can be part of. Our joy by nature must be limited, for we are finite creatures. But God is infinite, and His joy is that much greater than any joy we can have on our own.

We can experience that joy to a certain extent here and now, but in Heaven there will be no limit to experiencing it. *Entering Heaven will be entering into His joy.*

God's Joy in Our Obedience

And you shall again obey the Lord, and observe all His commandments which I command you today. Then the Lord your God will prosper you abundantly in all the work of your hand, in the offspring of your body and in the offspring of your cattle and in the produce of your ground, for the Lord will again rejoice over you for good, just as He rejoiced over your fathers, *if you obey the* Lord *your God* to keep His commandments and His statutes which are written in this book of the law, if you turn to the Lord your God with all your heart and soul. (Deut. 30:8–10)

We have already seen that the Lord rejoices in our salvation. In this passage, He is rejoicing in our obedience. It seems that prosperity is a byproduct of the Lord's rejoicing over us "if we obey."

What is prospered here? 1) All the work of our hands, 2) our offspring, 3) the offspring of the cattle, and 4) the produce of the ground. This prospering is how the LORD rejoices over His people.

All these blessings will happen, "for the LORD will again rejoice over you for good." But the condition is our obedience.

SECTION TWO

Our Joy in the Lord

Rejoicing for Those Going to Heaven

You heard that I said to you, "I go away, and I will come to you." *If you loved Me, you would have rejoiced because I go to the Father*, for the Father is greater than I. (John 14:28)

Here Jesus is trying to give the disciples a heads up. He is telling them that He will be leaving them, but then coming back to them. This seems to have made them not very happy. After all, He almost rebukes them, saying *they should be rejoicing for Him* because He is going to the Father. If they loved Him, Jesus said, they would have rejoiced, which apparently they don't, or at least not as much as they should.

This may sound cold, but when a loved one is on their deathbed, and we know they are going to the Father, if we love them, we will rejoice. Anytime a believer goes to the Father, we should *rejoice* for them, even though we do not rejoice for ourselves, for we will miss them. 1 Thessalonians 4:13–14 says, "But we do not want you to be uninformed, brethren, about those who are asleep, so that you will not grieve as do the rest who have no hope. For if we believe that Jesus died and rose again, even so, God will bring with Him those who have fallen asleep in Jesus."

Resurrection Joy

Truly, truly, I say to you, that you will weep and lament, but the world will rejoice; you will grieve, but your grief will be turned into joy. Whenever a woman is in labor she has pain, because her hour has come; but when she gives birth to the child, she no longer remembers the anguish because of the joy that a child has been born into the world. Therefore you too have grief now; but I will see you again, and *your heart will rejoice, and no one will take your joy away from you.* (John 16:20–22)

Jesus is speaking of His imminent death, when the world would rejoice and the disciples would be grieving. But the story does not stop there. We know what happened shortly after His death.

The disciples were seriously grieved after the death of Jesus. Here is where Jesus' example of childbirth comes in. Yes, the labor is hard and grievous. But it doesn't end there: the child which the pain is bringing will wipe away the memory of the anguish of labor. The joy of a child being born is many times greater than the pain experienced beforehand. In the same way that the pain of childbirth is necessary to bring a child into this world, *the anguish of the death of Jesus was necessary for the resurrection and the resultant joy*.

When Jesus sees the disciples again, their hearts will rejoice. And here is the kicker: *no one will take their joy away from them*. The disciples would go through the great sorrow of watching Jesus die. But when He rose again, they knew that He was indeed alive, never to die again. That joy will not be wiped out, because they know! They had seen the resurrection; there was no way the joy brought by witnessing it could be taken from them.

Here is a great truth of the Christian life: our grief will be turned into joy when we see the truth of the resurrection and its power in our lives.

Grief Turned to Joy

So when it was evening on that day, the first day of the week, and when the doors were shut where the disciples were, for fear of the Jews, Jesus came and stood in their midst and said to them, "Peace be with you." And when He had said this, He showed them both His hands and His side. *The disciples then rejoiced when they saw the Lord.* (John 20:19–20).

The disciples have wept and lamented; now they are hiding in fear. Then Jesus shows up just like He said He would, and they rejoice. Just as He said, their grief was turned to joy. And oh, what a joy that was! This was the joy that no one could take away from them. And gone with the lamenting was their fear.

Those of us who are Christians, those who have understood the wounds in His hands and side, those who have understood that those very wounds were payment for our own evil deeds, understand that *to know that Christ is alive and well is a great joy.*

Trusting and Rejoicing

Our soul waits for the LORD;
He is our help and our shield.
For our heart rejoices in Him,
Because we trust in His holy name.
(Psalm 33:20–21)

The fruit of trusting in the LORD is *a rejoicing heart.* Because of that rejoicing, the psalmist was waiting for the LORD. A rejoicing heart helped him recognize that the LORD was his help and shield.

Trusting and rejoicing seem to be closely linked here. The trust is very specific; it is trust in God's holy name. A rejoicing heart is not free-floating happiness; it is rejoicing *in Him.*

Paul said in 2 Timothy 1:12, "For I know whom I have believed and am convinced that He is able to guard what I have entrusted to Him until that day." Paul knows whom he has thrown his lot in with, and *therefore* he can trust Him. When we know Him, when we trust His holy name, then our heart will rejoice in Him.

Revived and Rejoicing

Will You not Yourself revive us again,
That Your people may rejoice in You?
Show us Your lovingkindness, O Lord,
And grant us Your salvation.
(Psalm 85:6–7)

In this passage, the psalmist recognizes that to rejoice in God, we need to be revived. The reviving is necessary because of our disobedience. Disobedience requires repentance. When we repent, the reviving comes from God, and the reason is "that Your people may rejoice in You."

The results of salvation/revival coming to the people are listed in vv. 9–11:

- That glory may dwell in our land.
- Lovingkindness and truth have met together;
- Righteousness and peace have kissed each other.

- Trust springs from the earth,
- And righteousness looks down from heaven.

Lovingkindness, truth, righteousness, peace, and trust are secondary effects of being revived. But here the primary reason for being revived is so that we may rejoice in Him.

Rejoicing in God is what the LORD wants us to be doing. But we cannot be in rebellion to Him and rejoice in Him at the same time, although we can *pretend* to be doing this, just like all great hypocrites. "Therefore repent and return, so that your sins may be wiped away, in order that times of refreshing may come from the presence of the LORD" (Acts 3:19).

Rejoicing in His Name

How blessed are the people who know the joyful sound!
O LORD, they walk in the light of Your countenance.
In Your name they rejoice all the day,
And by Your righteousness they are exalted.
(Psalm 89:15–16)

This passage is pretty straightforward. What are the characteristics of blessed people?

- They know the joyful sound.
- They walk in the light of the LORD's countenance.
- In His name they rejoice all the day.
- By His righteousness they are exalted.

The first half of this psalm is all about the LORD: His lovingkindness, His faithfulness, His being the Creator, His exaltedness, righteousness, and justice. Then the joyful sound is mentioned, which can also be rendered "the blast of the trumpet, a shout of joy." Simply, blessed people know the joyful sound that recognizes all the aforementioned qualities of the LORD.

These people walk in the light of His countenance (v. 5). This brings to mind 1 John 1:5 and 7: "God is light, and in Him, there is no darkness at all," and "if we walk in the light as He Himself is in the light, we have fellowship with one another." This means walking close to the LORD, knowing Him, and obeying Him.

This results in rejoicing in His name all day (v. 16). This is really hard to even imagine. To see through all our troubles so we can rejoice in His name seems the stuff of fairy tales or, at best, tales of the saints of long ago.

Walking in God's light doesn't mean walking in a rose garden. He never promised us one (as they say). Those saints that we so admire mostly had a rough time of it. But if we are walking in the light, we can see our troubles with His light rather than trying to see His light through our troubles.

Rejoicing in His name is not a cold devotion to the ethics of Christianity. It is *personal.* To know *Him* is what makes this rejoicing possible.

If we have this kind of mindset, then we will be exalted by His righteousness. This is a statement of fact. If we are that shining city on a hill, people will notice. But these blessed people have their eyes on the light of His countenance (which gives them great joy), not on themselves and their being exalted by Him.

Rejoicing in Our Maker and King

Let Israel be glad in his Maker;
Let the sons of Zion rejoice in their King.
Let them praise His name with dancing;
Let them sing praises to Him with timbrel and lyre.
(Psalm 149:2–3)

The people are rejoicing in their King, i.e., their God, their Maker, by praising the Lord with dancing, singing, timbrel, and lyre. There is a personal connection here, too. The sons of Zion are rejoicing in *their* King. It is not an abstract doctrine.

The rejoicing comes first, then the singing and dancing. It is very definitely not the other way around. They are not singing and dancing in order to work up some joy. We are enjoined to be joyful in our Maker and King, and based on that joy, we praise, dance, and sing.

DAY

16

Rejoicing in the King's Coming

Rejoice greatly, O daughter of Zion!
Shout in triumph, O daughter of Jerusalem!
Behold, your king is coming to you;
He is just and endowed with salvation,
Humble, and mounted on a donkey,
Even on a colt, the foal of a donkey.
(Zech. 9:9)

Though this is a command to rejoice at the coming of the king, the people seem to have rejoiced spontaneously when the prophecy was fulfilled (Luke 19:37). When Jesus rode into Jerusalem on a donkey, the people of Jerusalem didn't have to be told to rejoice; they just did.

But why were they to rejoice, and why did they rejoice? *They were rejoicing in their king's coming*, their king who was just and endowed with salvation, the One anointed by God, their Messiah.

Another very personal connection is seen here. He is *our* king.

Rejoicing in the Lord 1

Ephraim will be like a mighty man,
And their heart will be glad as if from wine;
Indeed, their children will see it and be glad,
Their heart will rejoice in the Lord.
(Zech. 10:7)

The context of this verse is the restoration of Israel. The tribes will once again be mighty because the Lord will answer them. We see here that the children are rejoicing in the Lord because of the events that they witnessed; they are not rejoicing in the events by themselves. They recognized who the source of the restoration was and rejoiced in Him accordingly.

Rejoicing in the Lord 2

Finally, my brethren, rejoice in the Lord . . . Rejoice in the Lord always; again I will say, rejoice. (Phil. 3:1, 4:4)

What trips most of us up on this is the *always* part. The point that is usually made concerning these two commands is that the rejoicing is not for the bad circumstances, but in the Lord. But that is a negative statement—what rejoicing *isn't.*

These verses are two positive commands to rejoice. Yes, it is a command to rejoice *in the Lord.* It doesn't actually say, "Don't rejoice in bad things, but rejoice in the Lord." This is not the point, although it is true, and a good distinction to make.

Imagine that you live in New York. This would be like if you emphasized *not* living in California, Nevada, Nebraska, Michigan, Florida, Maine, etc. However, if you emphasize that you live in New York, it goes without saying that you don't live in any of those other places.

In the command "rejoice in the Lord," the Lord is the object of the preposition *in*. The rejoicing happens in Him. If there is anything else you rejoice in (your status in life, your kids, your favorite sports team, your accomplishments), they are so piddling compared to rejoicing in the grace, majesty, holiness, goodness, compassion, righteousness, etc. that are found *in the Lord*. There is simply no comparison!

Our rejoicing is not in negative circumstances, but in Someone who is beyond all earthly problems. Rejoice in the Lord!

DAY

19

Fullness of Joy

I have set the LORD continually before me;
Because He is at my right hand, I will not be shaken.
Therefore my heart is glad and my glory rejoices;
My flesh also will dwell securely.
For You will not abandon my soul to Sheol;
You will not allow Your Holy One to undergo decay.
You will make known to me the path of life;
In Your presence is fullness of joy;
In Your right hand there are pleasures forever.
(Psalm 16:8–11)

The LORD's closeness to David is the cause of his joy. There is not just joy in His presence—there is *fullness of joy*. David had set the LORD always before him. The LORD was at his right hand. He was unshakable. As a result, his heart was glad, and his glory (often rendered as his soul or his whole being) rejoiced.

David is rejoicing in his very essence. "In your presence is fullness of joy" (v. 11). This brings back to mind how David expresses his joy in Psalm 43: "God, my exceeding joy." Fullness of joy is complete joy. It is not talking about joy filling me completely, it is *joy's fullness*. That is a whole lot more than I am able to hold. In God's presence, that is how much joy there is, a joy to the uttermost, exceeding joy!

SECTION THREE

Rejoicing in Salvation

Inexpressible Joy

In this you greatly rejoice, even though now for a little while, if necessary, you have been distressed by various trials, so that the proof of your faith being more precious than gold which is perishable, even though tested by fire, may be found to result in praise and glory and honor at the revelation of Jesus Christ; and though you have not seen Him, you love Him, and though you do not see Him now, but believe in Him, *you greatly rejoice with joy inexpressible and full of glory*, obtaining as the outcome of your faith the salvation of your souls. (1 Pet. 1:6–9)

Inexpressible joy! How can we express joy that is inexpressible? Perhaps you have seen a crazy beautiful view in the mountains or prairies or the heavens, and you try to describe it to a friend, and it just doesn't translate. Even if you have a picture of it, the breathtaking beauty cannot be captured. (When I use the word breathtaking,

I mean your breath is suspended because of the beauty of God's creation.)

In a similar but magnified way, the believers to whom Peter was writing had a joy so great that words could not communicate it. But what is really interesting is in what context this joy happens.

First, Peter has blessed the God and Father of the Lord Jesus Christ for His great mercy, for their being born again to a living hope through Christ's resurrection from the dead, that they have obtained an imperishable, undefiled, and nonfading inheritance, and that they are protected by the power of God through faith. It is in these truths that they greatly rejoice, in the salvation that God has provided for them according to His great mercy.

But Peter goes on to say that they were greatly rejoicing even though they were currently being distressed by various trials. Then he tells them why the trials were in fact a good thing. The trials to our faith will result in praise and glory and honor at the revelation of Jesus Christ. Going through trials is like refining gold—it is put through heat to remove everything that is not gold, making it purer and more valuable. When we hear stories of Christians who are experiencing trials such as imprisonment or death and yet are enduring, we can understand that the outcome is more precious and more beautiful than the gold that existed before the trial. Then we give praise to Jesus when He is made known.

In our current climate, when our rather small trials occur, we are totally stressed out. Greatly rejoicing in difficult circumstances is a foreign concept. If someone says they are rejoicing in a trial, we do not readily believe them. Do we believe Peter's description of these first century Christians?

It is in this Jesus (whom these Christians had not seen but had loved and believed in and were suffering for) *that they greatly rejoiced*, which joy was both inexpressible and full of glory. This culminates in the salvation of their souls, and that salvation is the outcome of their faith.

Rejoicing in Salvation 1

Be gracious to me, O Lord;
See my affliction from those who hate me,
You who lift me up from the gates of death,
That I may tell of all Your praises,
That in the gates of the daughter of Zion
I may rejoice in Your salvation.
(Psalm 9:13–14)

Earlier in this psalm, David speaks of past deliverances and how God is a stronghold who does not forsake those who seek Him. Here David asks the Lord to notice his affliction and be gracious to him. He recognizes that the Lord can lift him up from the gates of death.

But David's reason for asking to be delivered (besides the obvious) is so he may speak of His praises and rejoice in the salvation that comes from God. This was not to be in the privacy of his own home, but in the gates of

Jerusalem, publicly praising and rejoicing in God's salvation. His emphasis was not on himself, but on God and what He had brought about.

DAY 22

Rejoicing in Salvation 2

And my enemy will say, "I have overcome him,"
And my adversaries will rejoice when I am shaken.
But I have trusted in Your lovingkindness;
My heart shall rejoice in Your salvation.
I will sing to the LORD,
Because He has dealt bountifully with me.
(Psalm 13:4–6)

This is another Psalm where David is pleading for help from the LORD. He seemed in constant need of it, and you can see why if you read 2 Samuel.

In this case, the first rejoicing mentioned is on the part of David's adversaries whom he anticipates rejoicing because they have overcome him, and particularly because he had been shaken.

But David knew the tables would turn because he trusted in God's lovingkindness. His heart would rejoice in God's salvation, a salvation which, by the way, had not yet happened. He was looking forward to singing to the LORD due to His dealing bountifully with him.

Previously we saw that we are to rejoice in the LORD during difficult circumstances. Here David is still in the difficult circumstances, but he is looking forward to God's deliverance and trusts God so much that he is *rejoicing in the salvation before it happens.*

DAY

23

The Springs of Salvation

Then you will say on that day,
"I will give thanks to You, O LORD;
For although You were angry with me,
Your anger is turned away,
And You comfort me.
Behold, God is my salvation,
I will trust and not be afraid;
For the LORD God is my strength and song,
And He has become my salvation."
Therefore you will joyously draw water
From the springs of salvation.
And in that day you will say,
"Give thanks to the LORD, call on His name.
Make known His deeds among the peoples;
Make them remember that His name is exalted."
Praise the LORD in song, for He has done excellent things;
Let this be known throughout the earth.

Cry aloud and shout for joy, O inhabitant of Zion,
For great in your midst is the Holy One of Israel.
(Isa. 12:1–6)

This chapter overflows with thanksgiving, and that thanksgiving is combined with joy. The two easily go hand in hand.

Isaiah 11 is a wonderful prophecy of the time when the shoot will spring from the stem of Jesse, and the "wolf will dwell with the lamb . . .the lion will eat straw like the ox. The nursing child will play by the hole of the cobra" (vv. 1, 6). It goes on to speak of the remnant of Israel being restored, ending with "and there will be a highway from Assyria for the remnant of His people who will be left, just as there was for Israel in the day that they came up out of the land of Egypt" (v. 16).

Then come thanksgiving, praise, and joy that God's anger is turned away and in its place is comfort. That comfort is stated simply: "God is my salvation, I will trust and not be afraid."

God has not only become their salvation: He is their "strength and song." God is our strength, and He is also our song, and that song is not a dirge.

"Therefore you will joyously draw water from the springs of salvation" (12:3). God is their salvation, so they will come to Him joyfully to draw water from salvation's spring. Notice that there is absolutely no reluctance in coming to God.

Have you ever been so thirsty that when you came to a water fountain that was spewing out warm water you were still very happy? Now change that scenario to clean springwater bubbling up from the ground, cold and refreshing. When we are desperate, we are happy for any kind of water, but God gives us refreshing springwater. We draw such water, such salvation, joyously.

The rest of this short chapter speaks of the people's thanks to God and their witness of His deeds among the people, praising Him in song for the excellent things He has done throughout the earth. It finishes with a call to "*cry aloud and shout for joy* . . . for great in your midst is the Holy One of Israel."

This joy is not deep down, unexpressed emotion. It is shouted and cried aloud. When the Chicago Cubs won the World Series for the first time in 108 years, Cubs' fans shouted for joy in Chicago and everywhere else they happened to be. We know how to shout for joy when our team wins. How much more should we shout joyfully for all that the LORD has done!

That Day

And it will be said in that day, "Behold, this is our God for whom we have waited that He might save us. This is the LORD for whom we have waited; *let us rejoice and be glad in His salvation.*" (Isa. 25:9)

That day refers to the time when "He will swallow up death for all time, and the Lord God will wipe tears away from all faces" (v. 8). This is the final salvation. We will indeed rejoice in His salvation on that day.

The Joy of Freedom

Go forth from Babylon! Flee from the Chaldeans!
Declare with the sound of joyful shouting, Proclaim this,
Send it out to the end of the earth;
Say, "The LORD has redeemed His servant Jacob."
(Isa. 48:20)

The second half of Isaiah 48 is a prophecy of deliverance from Babylon. Leaving Babylon is a good reason to be joyful. As they were going, the Israelites were to proclaim to all the earth joyfully that the LORD had redeemed His servant Jacob.

It would be easy enough for them to keep their happiness to themselves among all those who had been exiled and were now free. But they are told to proclaim to all the earth, with joy, that the LORD had redeemed them. They were to give credit where it was due, and they were to do it with a certain emotion. This is not something that could or should be faked. They would certainly rejoice among themselves to leave the land of captivity, but *that joy, of necessity, was to spill out* when telling others of their deliverance.

So what are we to do since we have been redeemed from our *spiritual* captivity? We certainly can and do rejoice with our brothers and sisters in the LORD, usually on Sunday mornings. But you can also let the whole earth know (or at the very least, your whole world) that God has bought you out of slavery. The joy you have in your salvation should be evident in the way you speak of it. If when you share the gospel there is no joy in it for you, track down the root cause. There should be *nothing but joy* when you speak of how you were rescued.

DAY
26

No Longer Abandoned

How lovely on the mountains
Are the feet of him who brings good news,
Who announces peace
And brings good news of happiness,
Who announces salvation,
And says to Zion, "Your God reigns!"
Listen! Your watchmen lift up their voices,
They shout joyfully together,
For they will see with their own eyes
When the LORD restores Zion.
Break forth, shout joyfully together,
You waste places of Jerusalem;
For the LORD has comforted His people,
He has redeemed Jerusalem.
(Isa. 52:7–9)

In Isaiah 48, the people of Israel rejoiced because they were leaving Babylon. Here Jerusalem is being called to rejoice. The city which had been laid waste for a long time would no longer be abandoned. The watchmen of Jerusalem would see the exiles returning, and they would bring the good news to the people. They would announce salvation joyfully, declare that their God reigns, and shout joyfully together, for the LORD was to restore Jerusalem. This is God's promise of restoration and the joy of faith in that promise.

We can joyfully speak to those who don't know the LORD about what the LORD will do in their lives, of how He will restore their Jerusalem. Just think how good your feet will look! "How lovely on the mountains are the feet of him who brings good news, who announces peace and brings good news of happiness, who announces salvation" (v. 7).

How easy is it to have no joy in sharing the gospel? Many people would be glad to hear such news, but when we tell them, it is often apologetic and with no joy. We need to know how *good* this news is to those who have been left in the abandoned city of their life. If we know it, if we can get our brains around it, then our joy in this great good news will be evident. It is like telling a terminal cancer patient that a cure has been found. No doctor would be apologetic about that!

DAY

27

Garments of Salvation

The Spirit of the Lord God is upon me,
Because the LORD has anointed me
To bring good news to the afflicted;
He has sent me to bind up the brokenhearted,
To proclaim liberty to captives
And freedom to prisoners;
To proclaim the favorable year of the LORD
And the day of vengeance of our God;
To comfort all who mourn,
To grant those who mourn in Zion,
Giving them a garland instead of ashes,
The oil of gladness instead of mourning,
The mantle of praise instead of a spirit of fainting.
So they will be called oaks of righteousness,
The planting of the LORD, that He may be glorified . . . .
Instead of your shame you will have a double portion,
And instead of humiliation they will shout for joy over
their portion.
Therefore they will possess a double portion in their land,

Everlasting joy will be theirs . . . .
I will rejoice greatly in the LORD,
My soul will exult in my God;
For He has clothed me with garments of salvation,
He has wrapped me with a robe of righteousness,
As a bridegroom decks himself with a garland,
And as a bride adorns herself with her jewels.
For as the earth brings forth its sprouts,
And as a garden causes the things sown in it to spring up,
So the Lord God will cause righteousness and praise
To spring up before all the nations.
(Isaiah 61:1–3, 7, 10–11)

This well-known passage seems to be speaking to those who had been left in the ruins of Jerusalem. Isaiah was bringing good news to the afflicted: care for the broken-hearted, liberty for captives, and freedom to prisoners. Their situation was going to make an about-face. They would have a garland instead of ashes, a mantle of praise instead of fainting. They would be called oaks of righteousness and the planting of the LORD, that the LORD might be glorified.

The people's shame and humiliation were going to be replaced with "shouts for joy over their portion" (v. 7). The remnant that had been left behind in Jerusalem was really a sorry lot. They were the poorest of the poor.

Nothing was left for them. And now? They were to have a double portion in their land and on top of that, "everlasting joy" (v. 7).

Look at those two words again. *Everlasting joy.*

The chapter ends with the full reason for the joy. Isaiah will rejoice greatly in the LORD. This is greater than rejoicing because of relief from affliction. He elaborates with the next phrase: "My soul will exult in my God" (v. 10). Why will he rejoice and exult in God? Because God has clothed him with the garments of salvation and wrapped him with a robe of righteousness.

These words are over-the-top words: *shouts of joy, everlasting joy, rejoice greatly, my soul exulting, righteousness like a robe, salvation like wedding garments, garlands, and jewels*, all because of God, all to glorify Him. "So the LORD God will cause righteousness and praise to spring up before all the nations" (v. 11).

Rejoicing in the Savior

And Mary said: "My soul exalts the Lord,
And my spirit has rejoiced in God my Savior.
For He has had regard for the humble state of His bondslave;
For behold, from this time on all generations will count me blessed."
(Luke 1:46–47)

This is part of Mary's song of praise when she met up with Elizabeth while they were both pregnant (Mary with Jesus, and Elizabeth with John the Baptist). Being able to exalt the Lord and rejoice in God her Savior was no small thing for this young girl, considering how she knew her family, betrothed, and community could easily view her. She recognized God as her Savior, and her spirit could rejoice in that.

Rejoicing Because Our Names Are Recorded in Heaven

The seventy returned with joy, saying, "Lord, even the demons are subject to us in Your name." And He said to them, "I was watching Satan fall from heaven like lightning. Behold, I have given you authority to tread on serpents and scorpions, and over all the power of the enemy, and nothing will injure you. Nevertheless do not rejoice in this, that the spirits are subject to you, but *rejoice that your names are recorded in heaven.*" (Luke 10:17–20)

If you were casting out demons, if you had the authority to step on scorpions without harm and had power over the enemy, you would certainly rejoice, too. But Jesus told the disciples not to rejoice in that, like it was no biggie. We view these miracles in another league. But really, the fact that we sinners (base sinners at that) are recognized in the heavenly realms and have the right to go to heaven is the most joyful of circumstances.

Do we rejoice that our names are recorded in heaven? Do we rejoice in our salvation? I suppose we more easily rejoice when we can *see* things to rejoice about, and we don't see our names recorded, so the things we see get more expressions of joy than the other. It ought not to be this way. Think of what it cost Jesus to write your name in heaven. Our resultant joy should be of the humble variety.

On Our Way, Rejoicing

And Philip said, "If you believe with all your heart, you may [be baptized]." And he answered and said, "I believe that Jesus Christ is the Son of God." And he ordered the chariot to stop; and they both went down into the water, Philip as well as the eunuch, and he baptized him. When they came up out of the water, the Spirit of the Lord snatched Philip away; and the eunuch no longer saw him, but went on his way rejoicing. (Acts 8:37–39)

Here Philip obeys the Lord by approaching the chariot of a foreign dignitary and striking up a conversation. After Philip explained the Scripture, the eunuch believed, was baptized, and went on his way rejoicing.

Salvation results in rejoicing. We probably rejoiced when we were saved, but now as we go on our way, we might not have so much joy. This should not be so; we are still saved, and it should still affect how we go on our way.

Why is our joy diminished? In a nutshell, unconfessed sin brings our joy down. "If we confess our sins, He is faithful and righteous, so that He will forgive us our sins and cleanse us from all unrighteousness" (1 John 1:9). This is addressed in a booklet by my father, Jim Wilson, entitled *How to Maintain Joy in Your Life.*[1]

1. Available at ccmbooks.org and Amazon.

DAY
31

To the End of the Earth

"For so the Lord has commanded us, 'I have placed You as a light for the Gentiles, that You may bring salvation to the end of the earth.'" When the Gentiles heard this, they began rejoicing and glorifying the word of the Lord, and as many as had been appointed to eternal life believed. (Acts 13:47–48)

This happened in Pisidian Antioch when Paul and Barnabas were on their first missionary journey, shortly after John Mark left them. They had been having a great response to the gospel in that city. On their second Sabbath there, "nearly the whole city assembled to hear the word of the Lord" (v. 44).

As per usual, the Jewish leaders were extremely jealous and started contradicting everything Paul and Barnabas were saying. That is when Paul declared that the word of God was to be spoken to them first, but since they were rejecting it, Paul and Co. would turn their efforts toward the Gentiles. Paul was in line with Isaiah's prophecy, which he quotes, stating that the plan had never been for the Jews exclusively. Salvation was to be brought to the ends of the earth.

When the Gentiles heard the news that they were included in this salvation, they did two things: they rejoiced, and they glorified the word of the Lord.

That God is interested in saving us is good news; that He actually made it possible is worth rejoicing over. Those of us who have already received the good news need to remember that people may want to hear that it is for them, too, and when they understand this they will rejoice.

Joy in the Free Gift of Salvation

Therefore, being sent on their way by the church, they were passing through both Phoenicia and Samaria, describing in detail the conversion of the Gentiles, and were bringing great joy to all the brethren. (Acts 15:3)

After their missionary journey, Paul and Barnabas returned to Antioch and reported to the church all the things that had happened on their trip, mentioning how God "had opened a door of faith to the Gentiles" (14:27).

Then some people came from Judea, teaching the Christians in Antioch that they had to be circumcised according to the custom of Moses in order to actually be saved. The ensuing argument necessitated Paul and Barnabas going to Jerusalem to sort this out.

Today's quote happens on the way to Jerusalem. Hearing the story of the conversion of people who were not Jews gave the believers in Phoenicia and Samaria great joy. Joy had not been the response of those caught up in the observance of the law.

After Paul makes his presentation to the apostles and elders in Jerusalem, who apparently listened very carefully (15:12), James gave the decision. He references the Old Testament prophecies in saying that the Gentiles do not need to keep the circumcision law. However, they were to stay away from idols, sexual sin, and eating blood or meat from strangled animals (which would still have the blood in them).

The apostles and elders sent a letter to all the Gentile believers, disclaiming any connection with those teaching circumcision as a necessity for salvation. This letter was read, and "they rejoiced because of the encouragement" (v. 31).

Here is another good reason for joy: being encouraged. Different subjects can trouble and worry us when teachers start adding things to the simple gospel. It is a matter of joy that salvation is not complicated at all.

And All His Household

They said, "Believe in the Lord Jesus and you will be saved, you and your household." And they spoke the word of the Lord to him together with all who were in his house. And he took them that very hour of the night and washed their wounds, and immediately he was baptized, he and all his household. And he brought them into his house and set food before them and rejoiced greatly, having believed in God with his whole household. (Acts 16:32–24)

The Philippian jailer's conversion is a well-known story. Here I just want to point out that not only was he saved, but he went from wanting to kill himself to rejoicing greatly in a very short time. The reason? He and his whole household believed in God.

On a side note, in the same chapter Paul and Silas were "praying and singing hymns of praise to God" (v.

25), and the other prisoners were listening. It doesn't say that Paul and Silas were rejoicing in the Lord, but it is not a stretch to deduce that they were.

DAY

34

Singing Aloud for Joy

Arise, O LORD, to Your resting place,
You and the ark of Your strength.
Let your priests be clothed with righteousness,
And let Your godly ones sing for joy . . . .
"Her priests also I will clothe with salvation,
And her godly ones will sing aloud for joy."
(Psalm 132:8–9, 16)

This psalm is one of fifteen described as "A Song of Ascents," sung by pilgrims on their way up to the temple in Jerusalem. It speaks of some of the important aspects of this journey.

First, the priests should be clothed with righteousness. This was not always the case, but it should be that way. Clothing covers the body, and that should be our relationship with righteousness.

Second, the psalmist calls on God to let His godly ones sing for joy. The godly ones are those clothed in righteousness. Joy is a crucial element of worship, and it is a natural result of being clothed with righteousness.

In verse 16, God tells us that He chose Jerusalem for His resting place, He will bless her, and He will dwell in her. Then He says He will clothe the priests with salvation. Salvation's fruit is the righteousness that results in singing "aloud for joy."

Sometimes we hear that joy is a deep, almost hidden feeling, as opposed to happiness that is all outward and bubbly. We see here at that the godly ones sing aloud for joy. Joy will out! It can't be kept in, and it shouldn't be.

DAY
35

The Joy of Restoration

For I know my transgressions,
And my sin is ever before me.
Against You, You only, I have sinned
And done what is evil in Your sight,
So that You are justified when You speak
And blameless when You judge . . . .
Purify me with hyssop, and I shall be clean;
Wash me, and I shall be whiter than snow.
Make me to hear joy and gladness,
Let the bones which You have broken rejoice.
Hide Your face from my sins
And blot out all my iniquities.
Create in me a clean heart, O God,
And renew a steadfast spirit within me.
Do not cast me away from Your presence
And do not take Your Holy Spirit from me.
Restore to me the joy of Your salvation
And sustain me with a willing spirit.
Then I will teach transgressors Your ways,

And sinners will be converted to You.
Deliver me from bloodguiltiness, O God,
The God of my salvation;
Then my tongue will joyfully sing of Your righteousness.
O Lord, open my lips,
That my mouth may declare Your praise.
(Psalm 51:3–4, 7–15)

This is a wonderful psalm, much preached on and written about. King David had been busted by the prophet Nathan for his adultery with Bathsheba, the murder of her husband Uriah the Hittite, and the subsequent cover-up. This is his psalm of repentance.

In verses 3 and 4, David admits his sin. There is no longer any cover-up. He recognizes that his sin is against God and God only.

In verse 7, David asks to be cleansed. Nothing he or anyone else can do could achieve guiltlessness. But if God cleanses David of the guilt of adultery, murder, and hypocrisy, he will be whiter than snow.

In verse 8, David asks God to make him hear joy again, and he wants the rejoicing to reach his bones. When he was overwhelmed with his sin, he could neither hear joy nor rejoice himself. This is only possible after he is washed of his sins. This is also true of us. Joy is the first thing to go when we sin. We don't feel like rejoicing, nor can we see reasons to rejoice when we are knee-deep in unrepentant sin.

In verses 10–11, David continues to ask God to fix him, to create a clean heart in him and renew his steadfast spirit. He asked God to not throw him out of His presence nor take His Holy Spirit from him.

Then he asks, not that his salvation be restored, but that *the joy* of God's salvation be restored to him. When we sin, we don't lose our salvation—but we certainly lose the joy of it. We have broken fellowship with the source of our joy. The joy can be faked with Christian lingo and behavior while in public. News flash! God is not fooled.

Here is a fun part in verse 13. When the joy of his salvation is restored, David will teach transgressors God's way, and they will be converted. If we are in the joy of the Lord, conversions are a byproduct. *The desire to evangelize picks up when we are joyful.*

In verses 14–15, David once again asks God to deliver him from the guilt of murder. He recognizes that his salvation comes from God and his behavior deserved the opposite of salvation. When David is forgiven, he will joyfully sing of God's righteousness. Again, the result of forgiveness is joy.

Several times over, we see that joy is the "in fellowship with God" indicator. We should have joy in our salvation, but that is taken away when we cling to our sin. Repent and rejoice!

DAY

36

Rejoicing in Deliverance 1

The LORD is my strength and song,
And He has become my salvation.
The sound of joyful shouting and salvation is in the tents of the righteous;
The right hand of the LORD does valiantly.
The right hand of the LORD is exalted;
The right hand of the LORD does valiantly.
I will not die, but live,
And tell of the works of the LORD.
The LORD has disciplined me severely,
But He has not given me over to death.
(Psalm 118:14–18)

This joy is apparently the result of being saved in battle. In verse 10, the psalmist spoke of nations surrounding him. Then he speaks of the LORD helping him.

How does the LORD help? "The LORD is my strength and song, and He has become my salvation" (v. 14). The LORD is three things here: strength, song, and salvation. The LORD is our song, but it is connected to His salvation and strength.

This leads us to the joyful shouting in verse 15. Where? In the tents of the righteous. These all go together. Where the righteous are, there is strength, there is song, and there is salvation, all of which are found in the LORD. And there is joyful shouting.

Rejoicing in Deliverance 2

Then Mordecai went out from the presence of the king in royal robes of blue and white, with a large crown of purple; and the city of Susa shouted and rejoiced. For the Jews there was light and gladness and joy and honor. In each and every province and in each and every city, wherever the king's commandment and his decree arrived, there was gladness and joy for the Jews, a feast and a holiday. (Esther 8:15–17b)

The Jewish people were under a sentence of death due to Haman's scheming. Queen Esther sticks her neck out and effects the salvation of her people.

The result? The whole city of Susa shouted for joy. The Jews were delivered at the last minute, so "there was light and gladness and joy and honor" for them. Then a holiday full of gladness and joy was proclaimed for the Jews as the news of salvation reached each city.

When our salvation is physical, e.g., a close call in a car accident, we easily rejoice in the Lord for bringing deliverance. We are genuine in our thanksgiving. Let us transfer that same joy to other areas of our lives.

A Promise Fulfilled

Then Hannah prayed and said,
"My heart exults in the Lord;
My horn is exalted in the Lord,
My mouth speaks boldly against my enemies,
Because I rejoice in Your salvation."
(1 Sam. 2:1)

Hannah was the beloved wife of Elkanah, but she was one of two wives. The other wife, Peninnah, was jealous of the love Hannah received, so she gloated over her that she had children and Hannah did not. The passage says that the Lord had closed Hannah's womb and that Peninnah would provoke her bitterly just to irritate her.

So Hannah prayed. The priest Eli, seeing her and questioning her, promised that the God of Israel would grant her request. That is exactly what happened, and Samuel was born.

The passage quoted here was when Hannah was fulfilling her vow to dedicate this son to the LORD because she gave birth as He had promised. Now she rejoices to fulfill that vow.

This is the beginning of her song of thanksgiving. She is speaking boldly against her enemies, which from the story we understand to be Peninnah. Hannah has been saved from the disdain of the other wife, and she is rejoicing in that.

This may seem very worldly to us, but it is also a kind of rejoicing that we can understand. When the Lord turns our situation around, even though it has nothing to do with "spiritual" things, we know how to rejoice.

Also note how she was rejoicing when she was giving up that very son she had so longed for. There is nothing but praise here.

DAY 39

Taking It to the Streets

Be gracious to me, O Lord;
See my affliction from those who hate me,
You who lift me up from the gates of death,
That I may tell of all Your praises,
That in the gates of the daughter of Zion
I may rejoice in Your salvation.
(Psalm 9:13–14)

This is a prayer for God's grace with a purpose, a purpose beyond being delivered from affliction. David wants to tell God's praises in Jerusalem, "in the gates of the daughter of Zion." He wants the opportunity to both praise the Lord and to rejoice publicly in His salvation.

The public aspect is obvious when David says "tell of Your praises." He would not be praising God by telling himself, since he already knows. He will tell others. We understand rejoicing as a private activity—but David wants to rejoice *publicly*. This is something we would do well to practice. Praising God privately in our prayer life and rejoicing in what He has done for us in our hearts is good, but we should not stop there. Take it to the streets! Tell people of God's goodness and what He has done to make you rejoice.

Anticipating Joy

Oh, that the salvation of Israel would come out of Zion!
When the LORD restores His captive people,
Jacob will rejoice, Israel will be glad.
(Psalm 14:7)

This comes at the end of a psalm where David is lamenting the lack of godly people. "There is no one who does good, not even one" (v. 3). The people are fools because they say in their hearts, "There is no God" (v. 1).

David affirms, however, that "God is with the righteous generation" (v. 5) and that the LORD is the refuge of the afflicted (v. 6). With that confidence, he longs for the salvation of Israel to come out of Zion. When the LORD restores His captive people, then Jacob will rejoice.

This joy comes after after the deliverance. Today, we can rejoice in our salvation that has *already* been brought about. However, David anticipates salvation and knows the joy that is coming as a result.

Rejoicing in God's Presence

O Lord, in Your strength the king will be glad,
And in Your salvation how greatly he will rejoice! . . . .
For You make him most blessed forever;
You make him joyful with gladness in Your presence.
(Psalm 21:1, 6)

This is another of David's psalms of deliverance. This deliverance has already occurred, and he is praising God for it. First, David addresses how he is rejoicing in the salvation God effected. In the second verse, David praises the Lord because He made David's glory great through that salvation. The Lord placed splendor and majesty on him and blessed him forever.

Then David says of himself, "You make him joyful with gladness in Your presence." It is not the glory, splendor, and majesty bestowed on him that make David joyful. It is the Lord's salvation and the Lord's presence.

Rejoicing in Restoration

Oh, that the salvation of Israel would come out of Zion!
When God restores His captive people,
Let Jacob rejoice, let Israel be glad.
(Psalm 53:6)

The five verses before this plea are David lamenting the sad state of affairs: fools saying in their heart that there is no God; there is no one who does good, not even one; God can't find any among the sons of men who seeks after Him; everyone is corrupt and going their own way.

Then David expresses his wish/prayer that salvation would come out of Zion and God would restore His people, resulting in Jacob rejoicing and Israel being glad.

DAY

43

Righteous and Unrighteous Rejoicing

And my soul shall rejoice in the LORD;
It shall exalt in His salvation.
All my bones will say, "LORD, who is like you,
Who delivers the afflicted from him who is too strong for him,
And the afflicted and the needy from him who robs him?" . . . .
But at my stumbling they rejoiced and gathered themselves together . . . .
Judge me, O LORD my God, according to Your righteousness,
And do not let them rejoice over me . . . .
Let those be ashamed and humiliated altogether who rejoice at my distress;
Let those be clothed with shame and dishonor who magnify themselves over me.
Let them shout for joy and rejoice, who favor my vindication;

And let them say continually, "The LORD be magnified,
Who delights in the prosperity of His servants."
And my tongue shall declare Your righteousness
And Your praise all day long.
(Psalm 35:9–10, 15, 24, 26–28)

Once again, David is on the run. He is pleading with the LORD to save him and to not delay. About a third of the way through (v. 9), he declares confidently that he will rejoice in the LORD and exult in His salvation. The afflicted and needy need that salvation.

A little later, David goes into great detail about how his erstwhile friends had turned on him, repaying him evil for good (v. 15). Not only had they turned on him—they also rejoiced when he stumbled, having a party about David's fall. Their joy was not godly joy. "Like godless jesters at a feast, they gnashed at me with their teeth" (v. 16).

This state of affairs does not please David, and he asks God to be the judge according to His righteousness (v. 24). He asks God to not let his enemies do that kind of rejoicing. Two verses later, David asks more of God regarding those who had been crowing over him. He asks that they be ashamed and humiliated completely, clothed in shame and dishonor (v. 26).

But then David returns to the positive kind of rejoicing. Back in verse 9, he had declared that he would rejoice in the LORD and in His salvation. Now, after asking God to bring down those who rejoice in a nasty way, he asks Him to let them who are on his side to shout for joy. They will not only rejoice at his vindication, but they would do this by magnifying the LORD. God would get the credit. It is not simply, "Yay, our guy won," but rather shouting about how great our God is.

David says that he goes on to tell of God's righteousness and praise Him all day long as a natural outcome of the salvation he will be rejoicing in.

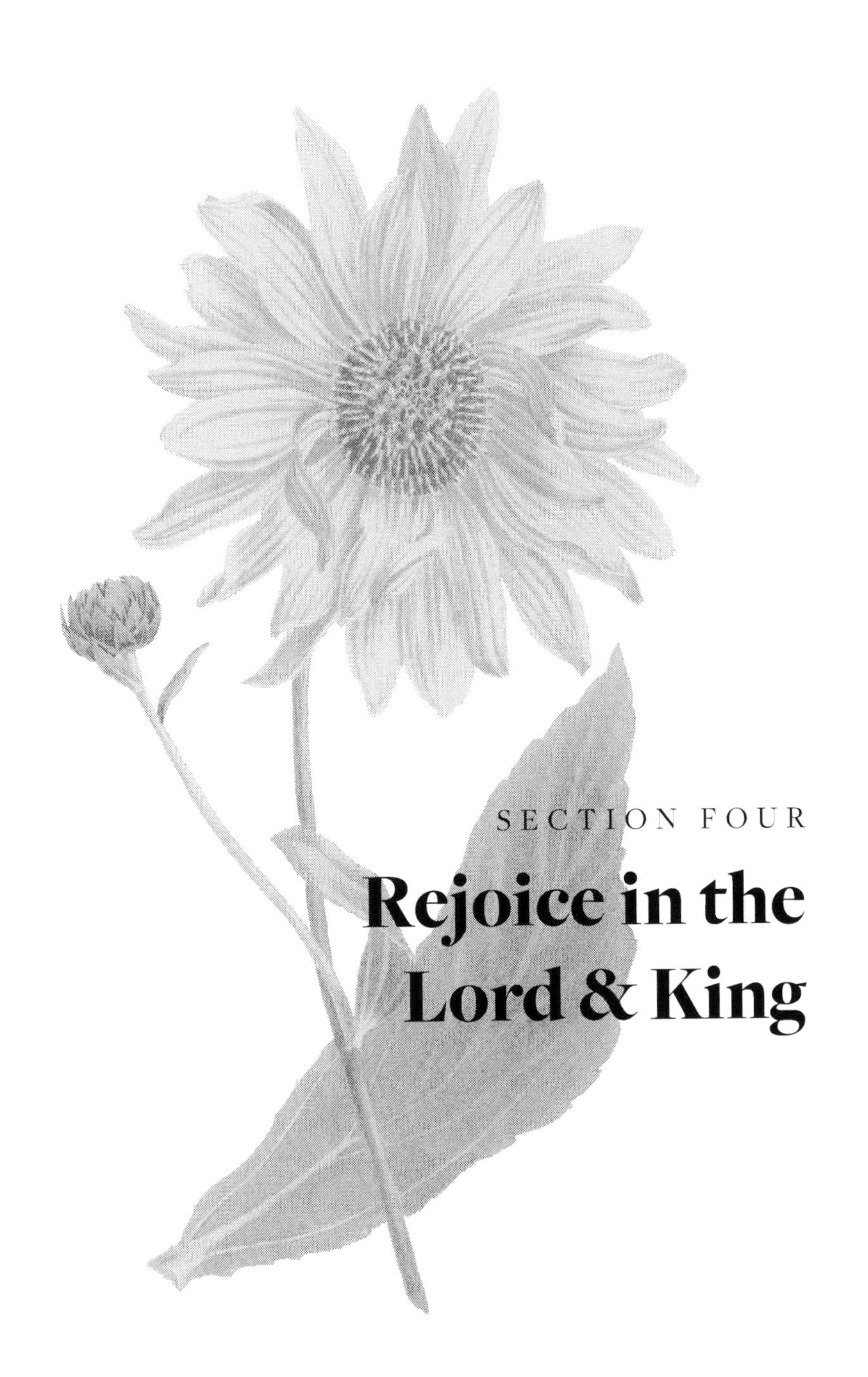

SECTION FOUR

Rejoice in the Lord & King

DAY

44

Contagious Rejoicing

I will bless the Lord at all times;
His praise shall continually be in my mouth
My soul will make its boast in the Lord;
The humble will hear it and rejoice.
O magnify the Lord with me,
And let us exalt His name together.
I sought the Lord, and He answered me,
And delivered me from all my fears.
(Psalm 34:1–4)

In this passage, David is blessing and praising the Lord, and his soul is boasting in the Lord. The humble hear David's praising and rejoice because of it. It appears that other people's praise can make you rejoice.

Then David calls others to magnify the Lord, to exalt His name, and to do this together. This will greatly increase the number of people who are rejoicing because they heard the praise of many and not just one. Perhaps this is why singing a hymn of praise to the Lord can cause joy to rise up in our hearts. Praise begets joy.

DAY

45

God's Protection

But as for me, I shall sing of Your strength;
Yes, I shall joyfully sing of Your lovingkindness in the morning,
For You have been my stronghold
And a refuge in the day of my distress.
O my strength, I will sing praises to You;
For God is my stronghold, the God who shows me lovingkindness.
(Psalm 59:16–17)

This is another psalm of David pleading with God to deliver him from his enemies. He asks God to set him securely on high in a place where they cannot reach him. The enemies have set an ambush and are attacking him. David asks God to wake up and help him (v. 4).

David likens his enemies to dogs who howl at night as they go around the city (v. 14). These enemies of David are prideful—they believe they are invincible. "Swords are in their lips, for, they say, 'Who hears?'" (v. 7). They are saying that they can do anything, and no one is going to stop them.

But David realizes who is really in charge. "But You, O Lord, laugh at them; You scoff at all the nations" (v. 8). David speaks with faith of how the Lord will meet him and help him triumph over these enemies. David asks that the enemies not be slain but scattered so they would be caught in their boasts (v. 12). He wants them to be treated in a way that people will know that "God rules in Jacob to the ends of the earth" (v. 13).

Then we come to David's joy, in contrast to the condition of his enemies. "But as for me . . ." David will sing of God's strength and sing joyfully of His lovingkindness in the morning. He says that his joyful singing will be about God and His mercy, His being David's stronghold and refuge in his distress.

This is a pattern that is repeated in many psalms: David is in trouble, again, and he pleads with God to come to help him. Then he recognizes that God will do just that, that he will experience God's mercy and protection, and he will sing joyfully as a result.

We also experience God's mercy and protection, but we may not recognize it. David had some very definite enemies in a political/warfare way, and we may not. Yet we can feel equally distressed or oppressed. Ask God for His strength, be held by it, and rejoice because of His protection. We should sing because of God's protection, but we need to recognize it for what it is.

DAY

46

In the Shadow of Your Wings

O God, You are my God; I shall seek You earnestly;
My soul thirst for You, my flesh yearns for You,
In a dry and weary land where there is no water.
Thus I have seen You in the sanctuary,
To see Your power and Your glory.
Because Your lovingkindness is better than life,
My lips will praise You.
So I will bless You as long as I live;
I will lift up my hands in Your name.
My soul is satisfied as with marrow and fatness,
And my mouth offers praises with joyful lips.
When I remember You on my bed,
I meditate on You in the night watches,
For you have been my help,
And in the shadow of Your wings I sing for joy.
My soul clings to You; Your right hand upholds me.
But those who seek my life to destroy it
Will go into the depths of the earth.
They will be delivered over to the power of the sword;

They will be a prey for foxes.
But the king will rejoice in God;
Everyone who swears by Him will glory,
For the mouths of those who speak lies will be stopped.
(Psalm 63)

In this psalm, *joy* is used as an adjective, noun, and verb: joyful, joy, and rejoice.

Verse 1 indicates that David is in the desert (literally), and he uses his very real need for water in "a dry and weary land where there is no water" to describe how his soul thirsts for God. This is a wonderful analogy: as we thirst for water, so our soul can/should thirst for God.

David then says that God's lovingkindness is better than life, and his lips will praise Him. Keep in mind that David is once again on the run from those who seek to destroy his life (vv. 9–10).

So as long as he lives, he will lift up his hands in God's name; his soul is satisfied with fatness although he is on the run, hiding in the wilderness. Because his soul is satisfied, his mouth "offers praises with joyful lips." We can offer praise in so many different ways (faint praise is one example), but here the praise is coming out of "joyful lips." It is obvious that David's joyful praises have only to do with God, and not his own circumstances, because there is nothing in his circumstances that calls for joy.

In verses 6–7, we see that when David thinks about it, he understands that God has been his help during his time on the run, and *it is in the shadow of His wings that he sings for joy.* Although he is on the run in the wilderness and having to stand watch, David knows the protection of God's wings, and he can sing for joy, for God holds him in His right hand.

David wraps up the Psalm by declaring that the king (David himself) will rejoice in God. He rejoices now in the wilderness; he will rejoice when he is back as king.

DAY

47

Awesome in His Deeds

Come and see the works of God,
Who is awesome in His deeds toward the sons of men.
He turned the sea into dry land;
They passed through the river on foot;
There let us rejoice in Him.
(Psalm 66:5–6)

Here rejoicing in God is a result of seeing His works toward the sons of men. The psalmist is presumably referring to passing through the Red Sea with Moses (Ex. 14:13, 22) and the Jordan River with Joshua (Joshua 3:13). The Israelites had the Egyptian army on their tail and a sea in front of them. The situation didn't look good. With Joshua, they were about to enter the Promised Land, but it was certainly unknown.

When we are in tight situations or anticipate difficult circumstances coming, we can be assured of the works of

God on our behalf, God "who is awesome in His deeds toward the sons of men." We can look forward to rejoicing after we reach the other side.

In verse 16, the psalmist says, "I will tell of what He has done for my soul." Even though God refines people through difficult circumstances (vv. 10–12), since we know that we will be brought through, we can anticipate the rejoicing, even if we don't yet know *how* we will be saved.

God is in charge! Let us rejoice in Him!

DAY

48

Let God Be Magnified

Let all who seek You rejoice and be glad in You;
And let those who love Your salvation say continually,
"Let God be magnified."
(Psalm 70:4)

This gem of a verse pops up in the middle of an imprecatory psalm. In the first three verses, David asks God to shame, humiliate, and dishonor those who seek his life and delight in his hurt. This verse is his plea to God to hurry up and deliver him.

In these three lines, there is a call to joy. Despite the surrounding verses, David is not talking about rejoicing *after* everything has calmed down. Although the circumstances are bad (he is being chased by people who are trying to kill him), he calls those who seek God to rejoice and be glad *in God Himself*: "Let all who seek You rejoice and be glad in You." Since they love His salvation, they are to continually praise Him: "Let God be magnified." Let God be enlarged in our eyes.

The praise comes before the salvation, but with an expectation that God will in fact save. His salvation is more than just a vague hope; it is a sure thing. God has done it before, and He will do it *again*. This brings to mind the definition of faith in Hebrews 11:1: "Now faith is the assurance of things hoped for, the conviction of things not seen." God's salvation is not yet seen, but there is faith that it is coming, and we can praise God because of it, sight unseen.

If we love God, it is possible to rejoice, no matter our circumstances. God is where the joy and gladness are found.

SECTION FIVE

Everlasting Joy

DAY

49

No Room for Sorrow

And the ransomed of the Lord will return
And come with joyful shouting to Zion,
With everlasting joy upon their heads.
They will find gladness and joy,
And sorrow and sighing will flee away.
(Isa. 35:10)

Isaiah 35 is about the future that is in store for Zion. Much joy is found in this chapter. In this section, Isaiah speaks about the ransomed of the Lord joyfully shouting as they return to Zion, their homeland. But it is not a passing, temporary joy. The kind of joy they are shouting is an *everlasting* joy.

When they come to Zion, they will find gladness and joy. This time, there will be no sorrow or sighing there, because they will have fled away. *Sorrow cannot stand before real rejoicing.* There is no room.

This was written to the Jews, but it applies to us as well. Many prophecies in the Old Testament are thought to have been fulfilled both near the time they were spoken *and* in some future time. The description of Zion as a place of everlasting joy where there is no sorrow or sighing certainly evokes thoughts of heaven. *We are the ransomed of the* LORD, *and our joy will be everlasting.*

From Generation to Generation

Whereas you have been forsaken and hated
With no one passing through,
I will make you an everlasting pride,
A joy from generation to generation.
(Isa. 60:15)

God gives us promises when things look pretty bleak. Here the people have been forsaken, hated, and avoided. In contrast to that, God promises to bring them pride and joy. Once again, the joy is not temporary; it will be from generation to generation, i.e., everlasting joy.

DAY

51

Garments of Salvation

Because the LORD has anointed me
To bring good news to the afflicted;
He has sent me to bind up the brokenhearted,
To proclaim liberty to captives
And freedom to prisoners;
To proclaim the favorable year of the LORD
And the day of vengeance of our God;
To comfort all who mourn.

. . . .

Instead of your shame you will have a double portion,
And instead of humiliation they will shout for joy over their portion.
Therefore they will possess a double portion in their land.
Everlasting joy will be theirs.

. . . .

I will rejoice greatly in the LORD,
My soul will exult in my God;
For He has clothed me with garments of salvation,
He has wrapped me with a robe of righteousness,

As a bridegroom decks himself with a garland,
And as a bride adorns herself with her jewels.
(Isa. 61:1–2, 7, 10)

Isaiah 61 is glorious with its promise to the afflicted. Jesus quotes the first two verses in Luke 4 to say that they apply to Him.

These and the promises that follow lead to the joy found in verses 7 and 10. The promises to the afflicted/humble include rebuilding of the ancient ruins; being called oaks of righteousness and priests of the LORD; and eating the wealth of nations.

In verse 7, we see that their shame at being afflicted will be replaced with a "double portion." In place of humiliation, they will shout for joy over that portion. To top this all off, everlasting joy will be theirs. This is not an isolated promise; receiving the double portion goes hand in hand with being oaks of righteousness and priests of the LORD. What we can concentrate on is being oaks of righteousness.

The contrast of humiliation and joy is stark. Instead of a continual state of being afflicted and humiliated, there will be endless joy. Can you even imagine a joy that has no end?

Between the two quoted passages, in verses 8–9, the LORD promises an everlasting covenant to their offspring. The joy and the covenant are both everlasting.

So we come to verse 10 where Isaiah states that he will rejoice greatly in the LORD, and his soul will exult in his God. Why? The LORD had "clothed him with garments of salvation and wrapped him with a robe of righteousness." His salvation and righteousness envelop him. That is why his soul exults in God. Isaiah goes on to say that his righteousness is like a bridegroom decked with a garland and a bride adorned with jewels. We associate weddings with great joy, and the wonderful clothing and flowers highlight that joy.

SECTION SIX

Complete Joy, Great Joy, and Full Joy

Renewing the Kingdom

Then Samuel said to the people, "Come and let us go to Gilgal and renew the kingdom there." So all the people went to Gilgal, and there they made Saul king before the Lord in Gilgal. There they also offered sacrifices of peace offerings before the Lord, and there Saul and all the men of Israel rejoiced greatly. (1 Sam. 11:14–15)

Israel had asked Samuel to give them a king because they wanted to be like other nations. Samuel warns them about having a king, but God lets him go ahead. He anoints Saul, at first secretly, and then publicly. Saul then goes out and defeats the Ammonites, after which we have this great celebration.

In verse 14, Samuel seems to want to inaugurate the kingdom properly, to "renew the kingdom there." So all the people go up to Gilgal, and this time Saul is made king "before the Lord." Sacrifices of peace offerings are offered before the LORD, and Saul and all the men of Israel rejoice greatly.

What is this joy based on? It seems from the context that it is due to 1) getting a king, 2) defeating the Ammonites, and 3) being all together making sacrifices of peace offering. Saul himself is rejoicing with all the men. They are all before the LORD and at peace.

An Uproar of Joy

Zadok the priest then took the horn of oil from the tent and anointed Solomon. Then they blew the trumpet, and all the people said, "Long live King Solomon!" All the people went up after him, and the people were playing on flutes and rejoicing with great joy, so that the earth shook at their noise . . . . "Zadok the priest and Nathan the prophet have anointed him king in Gihon, and they have come up from there rejoicing, so that the city is in an uproar. This is the noise which you have heard." (1 Kings 1:39–40, 45)

The previous passage concerned Saul being made king. Here the rejoicing is for Solomon being made king. There is no such party mentioned for David, due perhaps to the circumstances of his becoming king after Saul died in battle with his son Jonathan.

King David is still alive when all this is happening. In fact, he gave orders on how it was to be done (v. 32). There was some serious rejoicing going on: trumpets and flutes, and the earth shaking at the noise.

The anointing happened in Gihon, east of Jerusalem, and the procession came up from there, making such a racket that Adonijah, who had had himself anointed king by the priest Abiathar, asked what all the uproar was.

The key difference between the two contenders for the throne is found in 1 Kings 1:5. "Now Adonijah the son of Haggith exalted himself, saying, 'I will be king.' So he prepared for himself chariots and horsemen with fifty men to run before him." Adonijah was anointing *himself* king, even though he had Abiathar do the actual thing.

But Solomon had been promised the kingship, and his coming to power was directed by his father. He did not have to arrange the party for himself. In Solomon's case, it was "all the people." For Adonijah, it was fifty people.

Great joy is not contained, at least not in this account. There was order, but it was loud!

DAY

54

Quiet Joy

Then he brought the king's son out and put the crown on him and gave him the testimony; and they made him king and anointed him, and they clapped their hands and said, "Long live the king!" When Athaliah heard the noise of the guard and of the people, she came to the people in the house of the LORD. She looked, and behold the king was standing by the pillar, according to the custom, with the captains and the trumpeters beside the king; and all the people of the land rejoiced and blew trumpets. Then Athaliah tore her clothes and cried, "Treason! Treason!" . . . . He took the captains of hundreds and the Carites and the guards and all the people of the land; and they brought the king down from the house of the LORD, and came by the way of the gate of the guards to the king's house. And he sat on the throne of the kings. So all the people of the land rejoiced, and the city was peaceful. For they had put Athaliah to death with the sword at the king's house. Jehoash was seven years old when he became king. (2 Kings 11:12–14, 19–21)

To get the whole story of what is going on here, you have to read several chapters before this. In brief, Jehoram, king of Judah, was fighting Edom and died. His son Ahaziah became king. Ahaziah had gone to visit the other King Jehoram of Israel, when Jehu (a rival king of Israel) came and killed Jehoram. King Ahaziah fled, but Jehu caught up, and his men killed Ahaziah (2 Kings 8–9).

When the queen mother, Athaliah, saw that her son Ahaziah was dead, she promptly had all the royal offspring killed so she could rule and there would be no rival for the throne. But Ahaziah's sister rescued one of his infant sons, Joash (also called Jehoash) and kept him hidden in the temple for six years.

2 Kings 11 is the story of how the coup was planned against the false Queen Athaliah. She was evil; there is no other word for it. Having her executed was step one in cleaning the country. The priest Jehoiada made a covenant with the king and the people that they would be God's, and they proceeded to destroy all the altars and statues of Baal and kill his priests.

When the house of Judah was cleansed of idolatry and the proper sovereign was in place, "all the land rejoiced, and the city was peaceful." Sometimes there is much noise with rejoicing, but in this case, the city was quiet and peacful. This is one way to rejoice—quietly.

Joy Heard From Afar

And the singers sang, with Jezrahiah their leader, and on that day they offered great sacrifices and rejoiced because God had given them great joy. Even the women and children rejoiced, so that the joy of Jerusalem was heard from far away. (Neh. 12:42–43)

In the return to Jerusalem from exile, there were two glaring needs: restoring the temple and rebuilding the wall. Ezra and company finished the temple, and Nehemiah completed the wall. These verses describe the celebration after the wall's completion.

Notice the prominence of choirs and singing in this expression of joy: "Then I had the leaders of Judah come up on top of the wall, and I appointed two great choirs, the first proceeding to the right on top of the wall toward the Refuse Gate . . . . The second choir proceeded to the left, while I followed them with half of the people on the wall, above the Tower of Furnaces to the Broad Wall . . . . Then the two choirs took their stand in the house of God. So did I and half of the officials with me" (vv. 31, 38, 40). Singing is a natural expression of joy. "The singers sang," directed by Jezrahiah. Perhaps the crowds were also singing; we do know they were rejoicing.

The rejoicing of the people came on the day when the leaders "offered great sacrifices," but the joy came because "God had given them great joy." Nehemiah adds the interesting phrase "even the women and children rejoiced." Why that needed to be commented on is not clear, but it does indicate that *the whole populace* was involved in this great joy. It was so great that even the women and children were part of it. The joy was so great in volume from the singing of the choir inside the temple and the rejoicing of the populace outside it that the joy of Jerusalem was heard from afar.

The joy here is of two kinds: the organized expression of joy in the singing of the choir and the spontaneous joy of all the people. The common factor is that God had given them great joy.

DAY

56

And All Who Heard Wondered

And an angel of the Lord suddenly stood before them, and the glory of the Lord shone around them; and they were terribly frightened. But the angel said to them, "Do not be afraid; for behold, *I bring you good news of great joy which will be for all the people*; for today in the city of David there has been born for you a Savior, who is Christ the Lord." (Luke 2:9–11)

This is the most spectacular birth announcement of all time. Our Savior has come to earth. He is the Christ! He is the long-anticipated Messiah! He is the Lord! He is a baby! He is God incarnate!

This is not just academic information. *It is good news of great joy!* What do we humans need on the most basic level? We need saving. We always have and always will need a savior. So here is the final answer to our most basic need—news straight from heaven, delivered by a host of angels. "Have I got some news for you!"

Of course, when the shepherds first saw the angel they were scared silly (i.e., "sore afraid"). The angel had to tell them there was no need to be afraid, because he had some really good news for them. It was so good that the natural response was *great* joy. A savior had been born!

You can follow the shepherds after this revelation to see how they responded. They decided to hurry into Bethlehem to find Mary, Joseph, and the Savior baby. Then what did they do? "They made known the statement which had been told them about this Child. And all who heard it wondered at the things which were told them by the shepherds . . . . The shepherds went back, glorifying and praising God for all that they had heard and seen, just as had been told them" (vv. 17–18, 20). They expressed their great joy in glorifying and praising God. They were so overflowing with the news that those who heard it wondered at it.

When we have met the Savior and are full of great joy, it is natural to tell everyone and let them wonder what it is all about.

Joy, Joy, for the Savior Is Born

Then Herod secretly called the magi and determined from them the exact time the star appeared. And he sent them to Bethlehem and said, "Go and search carefully for the Child; and when you have found Him, report to me, so that I too may come and worship Him." After hearing the king, they went their way; and the star, which they had seen in the east, went on before them until it came and stood over the place where the Child was. When they saw the star, they rejoiced exceedingly with great joy. After coming into the house they saw the Child with Mary His mother; and they fell to the ground and worshiped Him. Then, opening their treasures, they presented to Him gifts of gold, frankincense, and myrrh. (Matt. 2:7–11)

Luke told the story of the shepherds and their great joy. Matthew tells of the magi and *their* great joy. From shepherds to magi, they came to praise and worship the Savior with joy.

The shepherds were at first "sore afraid" (KJV), even though the news was "of great joy." After their fear subsided, they went to see the things that the angels spoke about.

The magi, however, were on a long journey, one that may have begun about two years earlier, because Herod had all the boys two years and younger slaughtered "according to the time which he had determined from the magi" (Matt. 2:16).

It seems that the star had not been seen for a while, because it was after they came to Jerusalem looking for the newborn king and got directions from Herod that "when they saw the star, they rejoiced exceedingly with great joy" (v. 10). It was as though they were back on track to find the one they had been searching for these many months.

This naturally led them to the house where the King of the Jews, who had been born within the last two years, was with His family. The magi had left their home in the east because of His star, and their purpose was to come and worship Him. They "rejoiced exceedingly with great joy" because they could now do what they had come to do. They could worship Him, and they had great joy in doing that.

With Fear and Great Joy

The angel said to the women, "Do not be afraid; for I know that you are looking for Jesus who has been crucified. He is not here, for He has risen, just as He said. Come, see the place where He was lying. Go quickly and tell His disciples that He has risen from the dead; and behold, He is going ahead of you into Galilee, there you will see Him; behold, I have told you." And they left the tomb quickly *with fear and great joy* and ran to report it to His disciples. And behold, Jesus met them and greeted them. And they came up and took hold of His feet and worshiped Him. Then Jesus said to them, "Do not be afraid; go and take word to My brethren to leave for Galilee, and there they will see Me." (Matt. 28:5–10)

Just before this, the same angel had caused an earthquake and rolled the tomb's stone away, and the Roman guards passed out from fear of him. Then this angel tells the women to not be afraid. We know the news he gave them, and that he showed the empty tomb. Then he commissioned them to go tell the disciples.

This next phrase is so good. "They left the tomb quickly with fear and great joy." We know that the angel who spoke to them was fearsome. The Roman guards fainted so completely that they were like dead men. Even though the angel told the women not to fear, when they left the scene, they left with fear. But it was not only fear—they also had great joy! They had seen the empty tomb and had been told by this fearsome angel that Jesus would meet them and the disciples in Galilee.

Before they can get back to the disciples, Jesus meets them. Note that they were already rejoicing before they saw Jesus. He also has to tell them to not be afraid, which they already were because of the angel. The joy and wonder and of course fear must have been overwhelming. But they still had a job to do that had been repeated by Jesus, so off they went.

To be afraid and to be joyful are not incompatible. The more we understand that we are dealing with a great and wonderful God, the more fear we will feel. This same God sacrificed His Son, Jesus, and He has risen. This was for our benefit—so much benefit that when we understand this resurrection, great joy is a rational response.

Joy and Amazement

And when He had said this, He showed them His hands and His feet. While *they still could not believe it because of their joy and amazement,* He said to them, "Have you anything here to eat?" . . . . And He led them out as far as Bethany, and He lifted up His hands and blessed them. While He was blessing them, He parted from them and was carried up into heaven. And they, after worshiping Him, returned to Jerusalem with great joy, and were continually in the temple praising God. (Luke 24:40–41, 50–53)

Here the disciples see Jesus' hands and feet, proof that it was indeed their LORD who was back with them. But their joy here is tied to not being able to believe it. They saw the proof, but it was so great that they still could not believe it—yet because they saw it they were full of joy and amazement.

A very watered-down example of this would be if you were in need of something, but it was not possible to obtain it. Then all of a sudden you are given it. You can see that it is yours, but it is hard to believe—but you are still very, very happy about it. The disbelief and joy are compatible.

In verse 50, Jesus is ready to go home. He blesses them, and in the middle of it He is carried up into heaven. What do the disciples do? First, they worship. They had spent forty days with Jesus post resurrection; they know He is their risen LORD. He has blessed them, and they were going to need it, for they were in for some hard times.

They then return to Jerusalem with great joy. The worship didn't stop; they were continually in the temple praising God. Praise is the overflow of a heart filled with joy. Pentecost is still another ten days out, and they are filling the time with praise and joy.

We see here also a pattern for coming together with other believers to praise and sing for joy because of our risen Savior. Again, the praising and singing do not cause the joy; the joy causes the praising and the singing.

DAY

60

Rejoicing in the Bridegroom

John answered and said, "A man can receive nothing unless it has been given him from heaven. You yourselves are my witnesses that I said, 'I am not the Christ,' but, 'I have been sent ahead of Him.' He who has the bride is the bridegroom; but the friend of the bridegroom, who stands and hears him, rejoices greatly because of the bridegroom's voice. So this joy of mine has been made full. He must increase, but I must decrease." (John 3:27–30)

John the Baptist is answering his followers who reported to him that all the people were going over to Him "who was with [John] beyond the Jordan, of whom [he] had testified." John was not only not concerned, but *actively rejoicing* in this turn of events.

John identified himself as the friend of the bridegroom who rejoices greatly when he hears the bridegroom's voice. Jesus is that bridegroom. John has great joy in him, joy that he says has been made full, complete. There is nothing to add; it is perfect.

John knew what his job was, and he did it faithfully. There was not an ounce of jealousy toward Jesus. His only emotion seems to be that of perfect joy. There was apparently a short time when John was in prison when he was uncertain if Jesus was indeed the coming one, the bridegroom that he speaks of here; but Jesus reassured him with miracles: the blind seeing, the deaf hearing, the lame walking, the gospel being preached, etc. It was a satisfactory answer (Luke 7:18–23).

Do we rejoice greatly when we see Jesus exalted? Is our joy perfectly full? Because He is our bridegroom (the Church is the bride), we should greatly rejoice when we hear His voice. He speaks to us, not mystically, but clearly and often, if we would but read His word and listen—listen carefully. We should hang on to His every word. Rejoice! The Bridegroom is speaking to you!

DAY

61

Obedience and Joy

My Father is glorified by this, that you bear much fruit, and so prove to be My disciples. Just as the Father has loved Me, I have also loved you; abide in My love. If you keep My commandments, you will abide in My love, just as I have kept My Father's commandments and abide in His love. *These things I have spoken to you so that My joy may be in you, and that your joy may be made full.* (John 15:8–11)

This chapter is about being fruit-bearing branches because we abide in Christ, the vine. I have chosen this portion to quote because it chockablock full of over-the-top promises that culminate in His joy.

God the Father is glorified when we bear much fruit. This fruit in turn proves us to be disciples of Jesus. The Father loves Jesus who, in turn, loves us. We are enjoined to abide in, live in, take up our residence in, and make our home in Jesus' love.

The passage goes on to tell us *how* to live in His love—by keeping His commandments. Many people resist obeying commands because they think it is demeaning. But Jesus tells the disciples that we are to obey Him and abide in His love just like He has kept the Father's commandments and abides in the Father's love. If Jesus could obey, and it is not demeaning, so can we. Then we live in Jesus' love, and because He lives in the Father's love, we live in the Father's love.

Why did Jesus tell us about living in the Father's love? First, so that His joy would be in us, and as a result our joy would be made full. This is not a human concoction of happy feelings. *It is Christ's joy in us!* He will put it in us as we abide in His love. Again, this is connected to our obedience.

In Christ's death on the cross, we see His obedience and His joy. "Being found in appearance as a man, He humbled Himself by becoming obedient to the point of death, even death on the cross" (Phil. 2:8). "Fixing our eyes on Jesus, the author and perfecter of faith, *who for the joy set before Him endured the cross,* despising the shame, and has sat down at the right hand of the throne of God" (Heb. 12:2).

We want the joy without the obedience, but it doesn't work that way. Jesus obeyed to the uttermost! We are calculating creatures who weigh the pros and cons. This one is a no-brainer: *obedience results in being made full with His joy.*

DAY
62

His Joy in Us

While I was with them, I was keeping them in Your name which You have given Me; and I guarded them and not one of them perished but the son of perdition, so that the Scripture would be fulfilled. But now I come to You; and *these things I speak in the world so that they may have My joy made full in themselves.* I have given them Your word; and the world has hated them, because they are not of the world, even as I am not of the world. I do not ask You to take them out of the world, but to keep them from the evil one. (John 17:12–15)

John 17 is known as "The High Priestly Prayer." In it, Jesus prays to His Father as the crucifixion is drawing hear. Most of the prayer is for His disciples.

Jesus says that what He spoke of in the world was for a point—that these disciples whom God had given to Him *would have His joy made full in themselves.* Our joy, by nature, is limited. Christ's joy is not, and Christ Himself prayed that we would have *His* joy.

This prayer was not only for the twelve disciples and the women who followed Him. Jesus specifically asks it for us, too. "I do not ask on behalf of these alone, but for those also who believe in Me through their word" (v. 20).

Christ's joy! Not ours.

DAY

63

Joy, Amazement, and Answered Prayer

When Peter came to himself, he said, "Now I know for sure that the Lord has sent forth His angel and rescued me from the hand of Herod and from all that the Jewish people were expecting." And when he realized this, he went to the house of Mary, the mother of John who was also called Mark, where many were gathered together and were praying. When he knocked at the door of the gate, a servant girl named Rhoda came to answer. When she recognized Peter's voice, *because of her joy she did not open the gate,* but ran in and announced that Peter was standing in front of the gate. They said to her, "You are out of your mind!" But she kept insisting that it was so. They kept saying, "It is his angel." But Peter continued knocking; and when they had opened the door, they saw him and were amazed. (Acts 12:11–16)

This is a fun story. This particular joy could be defined as surprised joy or confused joy. Rhoda knew that what she saw was real, but "because of her joy she did not open the gate."

She rushes to the group of praying believers and relates the news that Peter is at the gate. Although the saints had been praying for Peter, they did not believe their prayers had been answered. They think she is crazy—and perhaps the extent of her joy helped with that impression. You would think that she would go back and bring Peter in to convince them, but apparently that didn't occur to her. When she kept insisting, they conceded that it was likely his angel. It took Peter's continued knocking to get them to open the door—and then they were amazed.

Rhoda's response was joy, but she wasn't believed. Very often, Christians can be "stick in the mud" skeptics. We pray but don't really expect an answer, or at least not a positive one. When someone we know relates an answer to prayer, especially with great joy or excitement, the more "mature" believers are condescending, thinking the happy one is a little crazy or perhaps is understanding as real something that is "only spiritual."

When the Lord answers our prayers, we are amazed. We might be joyful also, but we are *surprised*. Although she wasn't rational enough to open the gate, Rhoda's joyful response to Peter showing up was the correct response. God is so good to us. We should be joyful because *He answers our prayers.*

DAY

64

Abounding in Hope

Therefore, accept one another, just as Christ also accepted us to the glory of God. For I say that Christ has become a servant to the circumcision on behalf of the truth of God to confirm the promises given to the fathers, and for the Gentiles to glorify God for His mercy; as it is written, "Therefore I will give praise to You among the Gentiles, and I will sing to Your name." And again He says, *"Rejoice O Gentiles with His peoples."* And again, "Praise the LORD all you Gentiles, and let all the peoples praise Him." Again Isaiah says, "There shall come the root of Jesse, and He who arises to rule over the Gentiles; in Him shall the Gentiles hope." Now may the God of hope fill you with all joy and peace in believing, so that you will abound in hope by the power of the Holy Spirit. (Rom. 15:7–13)

There is a wonderful interconnectedness in this passage. The Jews and Gentiles accept one another, and Paul explains that this was the goal all along, not just a recent idea. He quotes Deuteronomy, Psalms, and Isaiah to support his point. First comes David speaking of giving praise to God so the Gentiles hear. Then there is a call for the Gentiles to rejoice with God's people and praise the Lord with them. Then, quoting Isaiah, Paul tells the people of One who will rise from Jesse's line who will rule over the Gentiles, not in a negative way but as the One in whom the Gentiles hope.

The passage is topped off with a blessing in which Paul calls on the God of hope to do something. What sort of thing does a God of hope do? Fill people with joy and peace. What kind of peace? Peace *in believing*. What is the result? Abounding in hope. We know that our God is the God of hope; now we see that we may abound in hope in the power of the Holy Spirit.

This is the interconnectedness: praise, hope, joy, peace, and belief. They are tied to each other through God and the Holy Spirit.

DAY

65

Joy in Difficulties

Now I urge you, brothers and sisters, by our Lord Jesus Christ and by the love of the Spirit, to strive together with me in your prayers to God for me, that I may be rescued from those who are disobedient in Judea, and that my service for Jerusalem may prove acceptable to the saints; so that I may come to you in joy by the will of God and find refreshing rest in your company. (Rom. 15:30–32)

Paul was meeting resistance from disobedient people in Judea. He asks for prayer that it would end so that he could come to Rome in joy.

Sometimes people can come through difficult times with a stiff upper lip or with much complaining towards God and others. But here Paul is asking that he can come to them in *joy*, despite the obstacles. He asks for their prayers that that would be the case.

DAY

66

Complete Joy Begins with Christ

Therefore if there is any encouragement in Christ, if there is any consolation of love, if there is any fellowship of the Spirit, if any affection and compassion, make my joy complete by being of the same mind, maintaining the same love, united in spirit, intent on one purpose. (Phil. 2:1–2)

Paul says *if* there is any encouragement in Christ. He says *if* there is any consolation of love. *If* there is any fellowship of the Spirit, any affection, and any compassion. If the answer to these conditions is, "Of course there is," then there should be no trouble in making Paul's joy complete by being of the same mind. There should be no problem maintaining the same love and being united in spirit and intent on one purpose.

We tend to get this entire flow chart back to front. We think we need to be intent on one purpose, united in spirit, having the same love and being of the same mind, and *then* we could be encouraged in Christ, have the consolation of love and fellowship of the Spirit, and be affectionate and compassionate.

Perhaps you are in a place where there are no other Christians of your particular brand. They are high church, or they are charismatic, bland, or too modern, and you are not any of those things. But there is no other fellowship, so you find yourself with them. You find that they too have experienced encouragement in Christ, for they have encouraged you with it. And lo, they have fellowship in the Spirit just as do you. Voila! You are indeed of the same mind, maybe not in the particulars, but where it counts.

Christ and His blessings are the *source* of these things, not the end. We want to get to His blessings by working out some agreement with other believers in mind, love, spirit, and purpose. No—start with Christ! This will bring complete joy to all concerned!

DAY
67

Joy and Fellowship 1

I thank God, whom I serve with a clear conscience the way my forefathers did, as I constantly remember you in my prayers night and day, longing to see you, even as I recall your tears, so that I may be filled with joy. (2 Tim. 1:3–4)

Paul says that seeing Timothy would fill him with joy. He is constantly praying for Timothy, and his prayers are thanksgiving to God as he remembers Timothy and his tears.

Christian fellowship brings fulfillment of joy, especially after time apart. For many, there will be no reunion until heaven, which we know is a place of joy. Then the joy of fellowship will take a backseat to the joy of Christ's presence and fellowship with Him. But the fellowship that we have here and now is nonetheless *real and full joy*.

DAY

68

Joy and Fellowship 2

What was from the beginning, what we have heard, what we have seen with our eyes, what we have looked at and touched with our hands, concerning the Word of Life—and the life was manifested, and we have seen and testify and proclaim to you the eternal life, which was with the Father and was manifested to us—what we have seen and heard we proclaim to you also, so that you too may have fellowship with us; and indeed our fellowship is with the Father, and with His Son Jesus Christ. *These things we write, so that our joy may be made complete.* (1 John 1:1–4)

John is making the point that none of his information is hearsay. "We have heard, seen, looked at, and touched the Word of Life." (This is like our expression, "I saw it with my own eyes.") This eternal life was made completely open (manifested), which they saw, testified, and proclaimed. This was all done for a purpose. What purpose? *So that* they also might have fellowship with them whose fellowship was with the Father and the Son.

There is a three-way fellowship going on here: first, John and company with the people he is writing to (it is a general epistle, an open letter); second, John with the Father and the Son; and third, thereby the believers have fellowship with the Father and Son. If A=B and B=C, then A=C. Right?

John says he is writing these things so that his joy would be made complete. How will that happen? Through his testifying and proclaiming, those who hear and understand will be brought into the faith and thereby into fellowship with God and others.

This is true for us as well. *Where you have fellowship with the Father and the Son, there is joy.* When others also have fellowship with the Father, we have fellowship with them, and this results in joy for all concerned. When someone comes to faith and therefore into fellowship, *we all have joy.*

In the rest of the chapter, John writes more about fellowship. "God is Light, and in Him there is no darkness at all. If we say that we have fellowship with Him and yet walk in the darkness, we lie and do not practice the truth; but if we walk in the Light as He Himself is in the Light, we have fellowship with one another" (vv. 5b–7a).

If there is no joy, we can deduce that there is a hindrance in fellowship somewhere. It is easy to say that we are in fellowship with the Father, but we are definitely lying if we are walking in darkness. Walking in the light creates the possibility of fellowship and thereby joy.

Joy and Fellowship 3

Though I have many things to write to you, I do not want to do so with paper and ink; but I hope to come to you and speak face to face, so that your joy may be made full. (2 John 12)

There is real and legitimate joy in being with other believers. John could have written a much longer letter than this, but he is hoping to see them so that they would have full joy. When there is no possibility of a reunion, letters are wonderful. But who wouldn't rather see the sender of the letter if there was a choice?

Joy and Walking in Truth

I have no greater joy than this, to hear of my children walking in the truth. (2 John 4)

Here John expresses what gives him the most joy. It is that these believers are walking in the truth. In 1 John 1:6, John equated practicing truth with walking in the light. In 1 John 1:5, he says that God is light. Walking in the truth, walking in the light, walking with God are cause for joy for our spiritual leaders as well as for ourselves. The goal is not the *feeling* of joy but walking with God. Joy is the *fruit* of that walk.

DAY

71

Blameless and Joyful

Now to Him who is able to keep you from stumbling, and to make you stand in the presence of His glory blameless with great joy, to the only God our Savior, through Jesus Christ our Lord, be glory, majesty, dominion and authority, before all time and now and forever. Amen. (Jude 24–25)

This is one outstanding benediction! What does it say about God?

- He is able to keep us from stumbling.
- He is able to make us stand in the presence of His glory.
- He enables us to do so blameless and with great joy.

Can you imagine standing before God's glory in Heaven? Standing there blameless? At the beginning of the blessing,

John says, "To Him who is able to keep you from stumbling . . ." Jesus and only Jesus can make us blameless.

This is what heaven will be like. We will be in the presence of His glory, we will be blameless, and we will have great joy.

Overflowing Joy

Great is my confidence in you; great is my boasting on your behalf. I am filled with comfort; *I am overflowing with joy in all our affliction.* (2 Cor. 7:4)

Now, brethren, we wish to make known to you the grace of God which has been given in the churches of Macedonia, that in a great ordeal of affliction their abundance of joy and their deep poverty overflowed in the wealth of their liberality. (2 Cor. 8:1–2)

Here *overflowing* joy happens in tough circumstances. What are some things that overflow? A river can overflow its banks. The sink, tub, or toilet can overflow. A bucket can overflow. David says in Psalm 23 that his cup overflows. What happens in each of these cases? What is within spills over the sides. All the surrounding land of a river becomes drenched. Whatever was in the sink, tub, or bucket will be what is on the floor.

So if our joy overflows, it means that anyone nearby will get splashed with joy. It means the joy in our hearts is coming out. In 2 Corinthians 8, abundant joy overflowed in the form of "a wealth of liberality." Usually, people don't like to be splashed, but to be splashed with another person's joy is wonderful.

SECTION SEVEN

Temporary Joy

Carpe Diem

Rejoice and be glad, O daughter of Edom,
Who dwells in the land of Uz;
But the cup will come around to you as well,
You will become drunk and make yourself naked.
(Lam. 4:21)

There are a number of places in Scripture that refer to joy that does not last. Earlier in this chapter, Jeremiah laments the fall of Jerusalem. He describes how bad the situation is with a before-and-after comparison:

> Her consecrated ones were purer than snow,
> They were whiter than milk;
> They were more ruddy in body than corals,
> Their polishing was like lapis lazuli.
> Their appearance is blacker than soot,
> They are not recognized in the streets;

> Their skin is shriveled on their bones,
> It is withered, it has become like wood.
> (Lam. 4:7–8)

The passage quoted at the beginning told the "daughter of Edom . . .in the land of Uz" that she would fare no better than Israel and Judah. The problem was not confined to Jerusalem; each of these nations was subject to judgment because of the sins of them all. It is as though the prophet is saying, "Go ahead, rejoice . . .*now.* In a bit, this judgment will be yours, too." Their "joy," if it can be called that, is only until judgment.

Someone may appear to be joyful because everything seems to be going their way, but you know they are riding on a fast train to judgment. Their "joy" will end when the comfort ends. This is so very different from God's joy.

The Momentary Joy of the Godless

Do you know this from of old,
From the establishment of man on earth,
That the triumphing of the wicked is short,
And the joy of the godless momentary?
(Job 20:4–5)

It is always a bit chancy to quote from the book of Job when it is not God speaking, because Job's comforters got it all wrong. Many of the statements are true—they just didn't apply to Job.

In this case, Zophar the Naamathite points out the obvious, that the joy of the godless does not last. Zophar turned this true statement to say that *any time* joy ends, it must mean there was godlessness involved. That is like saying, "Dogs have four legs. A horse has four legs. Therefore, a horse is a dog."

There was one thing in common between godless men and Job, and that is loss of joy. That did not make Job godless. The opposite is also false. If a godly man is joyful, and I see that another man is joyful, it does not follow that the second man must be godly.

But we cannot discount the truth of the statement that the joy of the godless will not, cannot, last. It is momentary.

Joy without Roots

The one on whom seed was sown on the rocky places, this is the man who hears the word and immediately receives it with joy; yet he has no firm root in himself, but is only temporary, and when affliction or persecution arises because of the word, immediately he falls away. (Matt. 13:20–21)

This parable is repeated in Mark 4:16–17 and Luke 8:13. The Luke passage has *temptation* instead of *affliction*. This is the Parable of the Sower, but the focus of this quote is on the soil receiving the Word with joy. The Word is preached, and there is a joyful response. All good so far. But there is no root, so the joy is temporary. It takes only a little trouble, a bit of persecution, and the previously joyful receiver of good news is nowhere to be found. He has disappeared like tumbleweed with no root to keep him in joyfully in place.

This is why many people are skeptical of mass evangelism. Many walk forward at invitations, in joy, to receive the good news, but it doesn't last. Evangelists know this to be the case, as the Sower knew not all His seed would land in well-tilled soil. That does not mean seeds shouldn't be sown far and wide or that mass evangelism is bad.

Instead of disdaining this type of evangelism, as children of the light, we should work on preparing the soil around us, removing rocks, thistles, and any other hindrance to the Gospel.

Material Joy

Now there was a rich man, and he habitually dressed in purple and fine linen, *joyously living in splendor* every day. And a poor man named Lazarus was laid at this gate, covered with sores, and longing to be fed with the crumbs which were falling from the rich man's table; besides, even the dogs were coming and licking his sores. Now the poor man died and was carried away by the angels to Abraham's bosom; and the rich man also died and was buried. In Hades he lifted up his eyes, being in torment, and saw Abraham far away and Lazarus in his bosom. (Luke 16:19–23)

In this parable, the once-rich man is reduced to begging as Lazarus had done on earth. He receives as much mercy as he gave, i.e., none.

How the rich man had lived on earth (joyously) is contrasted with how he was spending time in Hades (in torment). His joy was connected to extravagant living. It had no root. The godless rich may be joyful, at least in their comforts, throughout their life, but it will end, and there will be no mercy.

Christians can also be joyful for material blessings. And we should be thankful to God for those things. *But they must not be the reason for our joy.* If they were, Christians around the world who are suffering tribulation or are dirt poor would have no reason for joy. *God* is our joy, and He is the same whatever our economic circumstances might be. If and when our comfort is removed, see to it that the joy remains.

Fair-Weather Joy

You have sent to John, and he has testified to the truth. But the testimony which I receive is not from man, but I say these things so that you may be saved. He was the lamp that was burning and shining, and *you were willing to rejoice for a while in his light.* But the testimony which I have is greater than the testimony of John; for the works which the Father has given Me to accomplish—the very works that I do—testify about Me, that the Father has sent Me. (John 5:33–36)

John testified that Jesus was the Lamb of God. He was the man chosen to come before the light, to point out the light, although he himself was not the light. In calling people to repentance, John did not mince his words. Yet people flocked to him. He was a burning, shining light, and people rejoiced for a while in that light. Even the

Pharisees tried to give tepid support to John, although Jesus called them out on it later.

But Jesus' testimony was greater than John's. John said that he was unworthy to even untie Jesus' sandals. Jesus was doing the works of the Father, and those works made it clear that Jesus was sent by the Father.

The people's rejoicing in John's light didn't last. John was arrested, and so his light dimmed. The joy that people had in John's teaching was of the "fair weather" variety. Bad weather will come. Be sure you have the kind of joy that can weather a storm.

SECTION EIGHT

Joy in His Word and Works

Rejoicing the Heart

The precepts of the LORD are right, *rejoicing the heart*;
The commandment of the LORD is pure, enlightening
the eyes."
(Psalm 19:8)

The first six verses of this psalm are all about how the heavens declare the glory of God. Then it turns to declare the wonders of the law of the LORD. The Law of the LORD . . .

- is perfect and restores the soul
- is sure, making wise the simple
- is right, rejoicing the heart
- is pure, enlightening the eyes

Some of us find it easy to rejoice in the beauty of God's creation. Others more easily rejoice in His written law and commands, loving to study and meditate on them. Their souls are restored, they are made wise, their heart rejoices, and their eyes are enlightened.

There is room, much room, for *both*. We should not settle for just one way to rejoice; we should be joyful in both.

DAY

79

The Joy of Your Testimonies

I have rejoiced in the way of Your testimonies
As much as in all riches . . . .
I have inherited Your testimonies forever,
For they are the joy of my heart . . . .
I rejoice at Your word,
As one who finds great spoil.
(Psalm 119:14, 111, 162)

Psalm 119 is the longest chapter of the Bible. It is all about the Word of God. The psalm is weighted with words such as obeying, meditating, upright living, learning, righteous judging, longing, rebuking, teaching, clinging, and so on.

Psalm 119 is not, however, about the *rigors* of God's law. Recurring themes include treasuring, delighting, hoping, comforting, singing, loving, and rejoicing.

These three verses show how the psalmist saw God's word as a cause of joy. In verse 14, he says that God's testimonies give as much joy as all riches. In verse 162, he rejoices in God's word like one who finds a treasure. In verse 111, the joy is not likened to anything; it just states that God's testimonies are the joy of his heart.

How can we find joy in God's law like we would in riches? Riches are tangible. You can do something with them that makes you happy; you can be comfortable with no financial worries; you can travel and experience things you always wanted to. How can God's law compare with these things?

It comes down to what you value. Is it important for us to know what God thinks?

God created us, and He wrote the owner's manual. He has spoken to His people. He has let us know how to do things, how to think about things, who is responsible for things, where to look for answers, and on and on. So when we read the Scriptures, we should hear God speaking to our needs. *That in itself should be a joy.* Wrap your brain around the concept that His word is life itself.

Everything riches can give us is external. Riches can make you comfortable, but they do not *comfort* you. God and His word can do just that. Riches can make you beautiful of face; God's word can make you beautiful of *heart.*

When we understand this, His word, His testimonies, His law will be the joy of our hearts.

Feasting on God's Word

Your words were found, and I ate them.
And Your words became for me a joy and
the delight of my heart;
For I have been called by Your name,
O Lord God of Hosts.
(Jer. 15:16)

This verse is sandwiched between Jeremiah pleading for the Lord to remember him and exact vengeance on his persecutors and him complaining to the Lord that He had left him alone.

But Jeremiah had feasted on the Lord's words. They had become a joy for him. His heart was delighted by them. Why? He had "been called by Your name." Like David in the Psalms when he is hurting spiritually, Jeremiah purposely remembers the Lord's word and promises and delights in them.

God's word can be a joy for us, too. But something precedes this joy. "Your words were found, and I ate them." Finding God's word implies that you looked for it. Eating those words implies that you took them in and were nourished by them.

God's word is like a meal that nourishes us. It is not just a sugary dessert. But there is plenty of nourishing food out there that we might not delight in. Think of a meal that you love and are thrilled to get to eat. That is how Jeremiah viewed the LORD's words.

Let's approach the Word of God like a prime rib dinner. Let's eat it up, enjoying it, delighting in every bite.

DAY

81

Joyful Concurrence versus Joyful Obedience

I find then the principle that evil is present in me, the one who wants to do good. For I joyfully concur with the law of God, in the inner man, but I see a different law in the members of my body, waging war against the law of my mind and making me a prisoner of the law of sin which is in my members. (Rom. 7:21–23)

This part of Romans 7 is referring to Paul before he was saved, since he is describing someone who is a prisoner of the law. "Knowing this, that our old self was crucified with Him, in order that our body of sin might be done away with so that we would no longer be slaves to sin" (Rom. 6:6).

This does not mean, however, that the unredeemed man is blind to the wonders of God's law. He joyfully concurs with the truths of God's word. But this is in his mind only. A believer who rejoices in God's Word should not do so only in his mind, but in his body as well, and that means *obedience.*

DAY

82

God's Glorious Intervention

"And this woman, a daughter of Abraham as she is, whom Satan has bound for eighteen long years, should she not have been released from this bond on the Sabbath day?" As He said this, all His opponents were being humiliated; and the entire crowd was rejoicing over all the glorious things being done by Him. (Luke 13:16–17)

Jesus had just straightened a woman who had been bent double for eighteen years. The text says that the condition was caused by Satan. As usual, a synagogue official was indignant because Jesus had healed on the Sabbath.

Here is what is interesting: this official uses an argument against Jesus that you may have used or heard used in other contexts. He didn't object to the woman being healed. But why couldn't Jesus have done it the next day? "There are six days in which work should be done; so come during them and get healed, and not on the Sabbath" (v.

14). Apparently, Jesus thought the Sabbath was an especially good day to restore a woman's health. It was a good day to break the bonds of Satan.

I don't know if the teachers of the law had previously determined that laying hands on someone for the purpose of healing was defined as work, but they decided it was in Jesus' case. However, we see that "all His opponents were being humiliated," in contrast to "the entire crowd rejoicing over all the glorious things being done by Him." This wasn't the only healing taking place, this day or other days, and people were rejoicing about it.

When we see the hand of God performing wonders, our response is joy. Being joyful is not something you do, but something you *are*. In this case, it is a natural response to God's intervention on our behalf.

DAY
83

The Healer King

As soon as He was approaching, near the descent of the Mount of Olives, the whole crowd of the disciples began to praise God joyfully with a loud voice for all the miracles which they had seen, shouting: "Blessed is the King who comes in the name of the Lord; peace in heaven and glory in the highest." (Luke 19:37–38)

We usually think of the triumphal entry as the people rejoicing and giving God the glory strictly for the King coming in the name of the Lord. However, this passage states clearly that the people were praising God "joyfully with a loud voice for *all the miracles* which they had seen." The people recognized that Jesus was a king and that He had come in the Lord's name, and the miracles proved it. The Healer King was coming to Jerusalem, and the people could not help rejoicing.

The Pharisees tried to say that Jesus' miracles were due to Satan's power (Matt. 12:24), but the people knew better. Because the people were praising God and honoring King Jesus, the Pharisees unaccountably ask Jesus to rebuke His disciples (v. 39). The people so closely associating Jesus with God had incensed the Pharisees before. Now they ask Jesus to make them stop it. But Jesus wouldn't do it. The people needed to rejoice. If they didn't, the stones would (v. 40).

SECTION NINE

Joy in the Gospel

DAY
84

Christ Proclaimed

What then? Only that in every way, whether in pretense or in truth, Christ is proclaimed; and in this I rejoice. Yes, and I will rejoice, for I know that this will turn out for my deliverance through your prayers and the provision of the Spirit of Jesus Christ. (Phil. 1:18–19)

Paul had just been saying how his circumstances (being in prison) had advanced the gospel. In verse 13, he says that not only does the whole praetorian guard know the Gospel, but so does everyone else. This was partly due to other believers taking courage and trusting the Lord because of his imprisonment and "speaking the word of God without fear" (v. 14).

Has this ever struck you as odd? Paul was in prison for preaching the Gospel; therefore, the believers became *more courageous* and spoke the word of God without fear. You would think that Paul's imprisonment would induce fear. We get scared at the possibility that someone might raise an eyebrow at us or ridicule us. When we see someone lose their job for speaking the Gospel, do we step up our game? Are we *encouraged* to speak the word of God without fear? Is this a cause of joy?

Paul doesn't stop there. "Some, to be sure, are preaching Christ even from envy and strife, but some also from goodwill. [They] proclaim Christ out of selfish ambition rather than from pure motives, thinking to cause me distress in my imprisonment" (vv. 15–17).

This is where Paul says that he will rejoice because the Gospel is being preached. "In pretense or in truth, Christ is proclaimed; and in this, I rejoice." We hardly rejoice in another's preaching the Gospel if we don't agree with them concerning the end times or church government, or some other such secondary/tertiary subject. *Are they preaching the Gospel? Then rejoice, even if they are doing it for selfish reasons.*

Are you concerned about whether the Gospel is actually being preached? Here is a succinct expression of the Gospel: "Now I make known to you, brethren, the gospel which I preached to you, which also you received, in which also you stand, by which also you are saved, if you hold fast the word which I preached to you, unless you believed in vain. For I delivered to you as of first importance what I also received: that Christ died for our sins according to the Scriptures, that He was buried, that He was raised on the third day according to the Scriptures, and that He appeared to Cephas, then to the twelve" (1 Cor. 15:1–5). If this is proclaimed, the Gospel is proclaimed, and we should rejoice!

DAY
85

Growth & Joy

Convinced of this, I know that I will remain and continue with you all *for your progress and joy in the faith.* (Phil. 1:25)

In the previous passage, Paul rejoiced in the preaching of the Gospel because he knew it would turn out for his deliverance, which could mean his death. In Philippians 1:21, Paul says, "For to me, to live is Christ and to die is gain." Win, win. To die means to be with Christ; to live means fruitful labor for him.

He decides in verse 24, "Yet to remain on in the flesh is more necessary for your sake." In what way was is it "more necessary" that Paul remain in the flesh? "I know that I will remain and continue with you all *for your progress and joy in the faith.*"

Progress in the faith and joy in the faith go hand in hand. The more we grow in the Lord, the more joy we have in the Lord. That is why Paul chose to remain in the flesh—for their progress in joy and faith.

DAY

86

Witnessing His Grace

Then when [Barnabas] arrived and witnessed the grace of God, he rejoiced and began to encourage them all with resolute heart to remain true to the Lord; for he was a good man, and full of the Holy Spirit and of faith. And considerable numbers were brought to the Lord. (Acts 11:23–24)

We don't know much about Barnabas, but what we do know is all good.

In this passage, the believers had been scattered because of the persecution that occurred after Stephen's death. They spoke the word to no one, except to Jews alone. But some believers from Cyprus and Cyrene had come to Antioch and were preaching the Lord Jesus to the Greeks. A large number believed and turned to the Lord (v. 21).

The news got to Jerusalem about this further development, but it was not the first they'd heard of it. The leadership in Jerusalem had already responded to the first Gentile believer, Cornelius. "Well then, God has granted to the Gentiles also the repentance that leads to life" (Acts 11:18).

So to be on the safe side, the church of Jerusalem sent Barnabas to check out the situation. What did Barnabas witness there in Antioch? He witnessed the grace of God, and when he did so he rejoiced. What other response can there be when you witness God's grace in someone's life?

DAY

87

With Their Whole Heart

Now when Asa heard these words and the prophecy which Azariah the son of Oded the prophet spoke, he took courage and removed the abominable idols from all the land of Judah and Benjamin and from the cities which he had captured in the hill country of Ephraim. He then restored the altar of the LORD which was in front of the porch of the LORD . . . . So they assembled at Jerusalem in the third month of the fifteenth year of Asa's reign . . . . They entered into the covenant to seek the LORD God of their fathers with all their heart and soul . . . . Moreover, they made an oath to the LORD with a loud voice, with shouting, with trumpets, and with horns. *All Judah rejoiced concerning the oath*, for they had sworn with their whole heart and had sought Him earnestly, and He let them find Him. So the LORD gave them rest on every side. (2 Chron. 15:8, 10, 12, 14–15)

Asa was the third king of Judah after the divided kingdom. He was the grandson of Rehoboam; his father Abijah had defeated Jeroboam of Israel. When Asa came to the throne, there had been ten years of peace in Judah.

Asa was one of the good kings of Judah, and that meant getting rid of the pagan altars, high places, sacred pillars, and Asherim, which he did. Then he ordered the people "to seek the LORD God of their fathers and observe the law and the commandment" (2 Chron. 14:4).

When the Ethiopians came against Judah in battle, Asa called on the LORD, recognizing that He was the source of victory. The prophet Azariah came forward to tell Asa basically, "So far, so good." "If you seek Him, He will let you find Him; but if you forsake Him, He will forsake you" (15:2). He went on to say, "But you, be strong and do not lose courage, for there is reward for your work" (v. 7).

Asa rallied the troops, restored the altar of the Lord, gathered the people in Jerusalem, and began sacrificing oxen and sheep. Then "they entered into the covenant to seek the LORD God of their fathers with all their heart and soul," and "they made an oath to the LORD with a loud voice, with shouting, with trumpets, and with horns" (vv. 12, 14).

Then "all Judah rejoiced concerning the oath, for they had sworn with their whole heart and had sought Him earnestly, and He let them find Him" (v. 15). The people turn to the LORD with all their heart and soul. They sought the LORD earnestly, and they were joyful about it.

Considering much of the history of Judah, they had been doing pretty well. There was peace in the land, and the idol worship was removed. But that is not the same as seeking the Lord with a whole heart and turning to Him. When they did seek Him, there was joy. "All Judah rejoiced concerning the oath."

Repentance without Regret

But God, who comforts the depressed, comforted us by the coming of Titus; and not only by his coming, but also by the comfort with which he was comforted in you, as he reported to us your longing, your mourning, your zeal for me; so that I rejoiced even more. For though I caused you sorrow by my letter, I do not regret it; though I did regret it—for I see that that letter caused you sorrow, though only for a while—*I now rejoice, not that you were made sorrowful, but that you were made sorrowful to the point of repentance*; for you were made sorrowful according to the will of God, so that you might not suffer loss in anything through us. For the sorrow that is according to the will of God produces a repentance without regret, leading to salvation, but the sorrow of the world produces death. (2 Cor. 7:6–10)

In this short passage, we see *sorrow*, *joy*, *comfort*, and *regret* in close proximity. First, Paul is comforted by the coming of Titus and the word he brought back from the church in Corinth, for Titus had been comforted by them. Due to the intensity of the first letter to this church, it seems from verse 8 that Paul regretted the sorrow that letter had brought them—although at the same time he didn't regret it because of the report he got from Titus that they still longed for Paul and had a zeal for him. So this caused Paul to rejoice, even though it was at the other end of some intense correction.

The Corinthians' response to Paul's correction indicated that although they were made sorrowful, it was to the point of repentance. This is the kind of sorrow that is according to the will of God. This is the sorrow that turns to joy, the sorrow that has no regret.

An easy analogy is in terms of treatment for cancer. As a doctor, you regret to tell a patient that they need surgery. The procedure is painful, yet it brings healing in the end. Paul wrote to the Corinthians like a doctor telling them they had cancer in their midst and it had to be dealt with posthaste. They did, and that brought joy to Paul, especially since he was sorry that such measures had been necessary.

DAY

89

When the Lost Are Found

And he said to him, "Son, you have always been with me, and all that is mine is yours. But we had to celebrate and rejoice, for this brother of yours was dead and has begun to live, and was lost and has been found." (Luke 15:31–32)

We studied this passage earlier in reference to how God is joyful when a sinner repents. Here I want to emphasize that there is joy in repentance for *others* besides our heavenly Father. The prodigal's father tells his other son that it is right to celebrate and rejoice when a sinner returns.

We know this from experience when someone close to us repents. We enjoy hearing testimonies of how, why, where, and when it happened. It brings us joy, as it should, for they were dead and now live, they were lost and are now found.

SECTION TEN

Joy in Service and Suffering

Joy and Comfort

Indeed, the LORD will comfort Zion;
He will comfort all her waste places.
And her wilderness He will make like Eden,
And her desert like the garden of the LORD;
Joy and gladness will be found in her,
Thanksgiving and sound of a melody.
(Isa. 51:3)

This chapter begins with, "Listen to me, you who pursue righteousness, who seek the LORD." So we know the audience of this passage; it is a promise to those who seek the LORD and pursue righteousness. The LORD will comfort them and also restore them to a place like Eden.

A byproduct of the comfort promised here is joy and gladness, thanksgiving and song. Joy is a direct result of the LORD's comfort.

DAY
91

Joy and Mockery

But he who kills an ox is like one who slays a man;
He who sacrifices a lamb is like the one who breaks a dog's neck;
He who offers a grain offering is like one who offers swine's blood;
He who burns incense is like the one who blesses an idol,
As they have chosen their own ways,
And their soul delights in the abominations.

. . . .

Hear the word of the LORD, you who tremble at His word:
"Your brothers who hate you, who exclude you for My name's sake,
Have said, 'Let the LORD be glorified, that we may see your joy."
But they will be put to shame.
(Isa. 66:3, 5)

Isaiah is lambasting people who were hypocrites in the extreme. God had a *low view* of their religious practices, even though they were making offerings to Him and not to Baal or Molech.

These people are mocking those who "tremble at His word." These are excluding real believers from worship.

It brings to mind how Jesus was mocked at His crucifixion. "He saved others; He cannot save Himself. Let this Christ, the King of Israel, now come down from the cross, so that we may see and believe!" (Mark 15:31–32).

In both cases, the mockers are not really interested in a positive response. Would they have repented on seeing those they were mocking rejoice? No, no more than those who drove Christ to His death would have believed if He had come down from the cross.

Still, as believers, there is always a reason to rejoice. Daniel prayed openly despite the opposition he faced. We can rejoice even if we are mocked.

DAY

92

Giving for Joy

Then the people rejoiced because they had offered so willingly, for they made their offering to the LORD with a whole heart, and King David also rejoiced greatly . . . . "Since I know, O my God, that You try the heart and delight in uprightness, I, in the integrity of my heart, have willingly offered all these things; so now with joy I have seen Your people who are present here make their offerings willingly to You." (1 Chron. 29:9, 17)

King David wanted to build a temple to the LORD, but he was told that he could not, due to being a man of war. It was left to his son Solomon to do the honors. In this speech to the entire assembly near the end of his reign, David tells the people that he had been laying aside great wealth for the building of the temple. In verse 2, he mentions some of those things: 3,000 talents of gold, 7,000 talents of silver, bronze, iron, wood, onyx, and other varieties of stone, precious stones, and alabaster.

This inspired the rulers of the fathers' households, the princes of the tribes of Israel, and the commanders of thousands and hundreds, with the overseers over the king's work, to willingly offer hundreds of thousands of pounds of their own gold, silver, brass, and iron.

This amount of precious metals could have been collected forcibly, but King David led by example, and the people followed. This is where the joy comes in. On the whole, *no one* rejoices about paying taxes, no matter what the money goes to. But here "the people rejoiced because they had offered so willingly," and King David also rejoiced greatly.

Next, David prays, again mentioning that he offered all these things willingly, and he adds that he saw with joy that God's people did the same.

There is no joy in being forced to give anything to anyone, even to God. But when you give with a willing heart, the giving is a cause of joy. And God loves this. "Now this I say, he who sows sparingly will also reap sparingly, and he who sows bountifully will also reap bountifully. Each one must do just as he has purposed in his heart, not grudgingly or under compulsion, for God loves a cheerful giver" (2 Cor. 9:6–7).

DAY

93

Joy in Victory

May He grant you your heart's desire
And fulfill all your counsel!
We will sing for joy over your victory,
And in the name of our God we will set up our banners.
May the Lord fulfill all your petitions.
(Psalm 20:4–5)

David is praying for victory over his enemies. In verses 1–4, he prays that the Lord would do the following:

- May the Lord answer you in your day of trouble.
- May the name of the God of Jacob set you securely on high.
- May He remember all your offerings, finding them acceptable.
- May He grant you your heart's desire and fulfill your counsel.

Then comes a great statement of faith that these prayers will be answered: "We will sing for joy over your victory" (v. 4).

David goes on with assurance in verses 6–9:

- Now I know that the LORD saves His anointed.
- He will answer him from His holy heaven.
- We will boast in the name of the LORD.
- May the King answer us in the day we call.

There is joy in being saved, and there is joy in being victorious.

DAY

94

Remembering Victory

It happened as they were coming, when David returned from killing the Philistine, that the women came out of all the cities of Israel, singing and dancing, to meet King Saul, with tambourines, with joy, and with musical instruments. The women sang as they played, and said, "Saul has slain his thousands, and David his ten thousands." (1 Sam. 18:6)

For [David] took his life in his hand and struck the Philistine, and the Lord brought about a great deliverance for all Israel; you saw it and rejoiced. Why then will you sin against innocent blood by putting David to death without a cause? (1 Sam. 19:5)

In 1 Samuel 18, there is serious rejoicing going on: singing and dancing with tambourines and musical instruments and joy.

Joy at the end of war is normal and good, especially if you have won, which was the case with King Saul and David after having sorted out the Philistines. We may not have experienced this joy in our recent wars, perhaps since they are all drawn-out affairs, but think how the U.S. rejoiced at the end of World War II. Millions of people hit the streets just as the women of King Saul's and David's time did. There was much rejoicing all over the world.

But that joy came at an awful price! Sixty million people lost their lives in that war. Joy in victory is that much greater when the cost is so high. On the non-victorious side, there is more relief than joy. So the women were singing and dancing with joy because their leaders had the victory. They understood that that meant many had died, but also that the dying was over.

In the second passage, Jonathan is trying to talk his father out of killing David because of that same victory. He reminds his father how David had risked his life to strike the Philistines and bring a great deliverance with the Lord's help. He reminds King Saul, "You saw it and rejoiced." Jonathan had to remind his father of the joy he had in their victory. "Remember? We won, thanks largely to David. You rejoiced then. Don't spoil it by killing your servant in a fit of jealousy now. Remember the victory, remember the joy."

There are many times when we rejoice, but then when we "come back to earth," we forget the cause of the joy and return to a state of no joy. "My brothers, this should not be so" (James 3:10).

DAY 95

God's Justice

The righteous will rejoice when he sees the vengeance;
He will wash his feet in the blood of the wicked.
And men will say, "Surely there is a reward for the righteous;
Surely there is a God who judges the earth!"
(Psalm 58:10–11)

In the first five verses of this psalm, David speaks to the wicked about how they are violent, liars, venomous snakes, and workers of unrighteousness. In verses 6–9, he asks God to deal with them: shatter their teeth, let them flow away like water, melt away like snails, and be swept away in a whirlwind.

When this happens to the wicked, the righteous will rejoice. Their joy is in God who judges the earth. There is a point to being righteous, even when sometimes it seems like there isn't. God said that vengeance is His. When He doles it out, it is just, and we can rejoice.

DAY

96

Tribulation, Temptation, and Obedience

Would that God were willing to crush me,
That He would loose His hand and cut me off!
But it is still my consolation,
And I rejoice in unsparing pain,
That I have not denied the words of the Holy One.
(Job 6:9–10)

Job had a rough time of it. He was feeling misused, to say the least. Misused and misunderstood. There was to be no help from his friends, apparently. He was so miserable that he wanted God to go ahead and cut him off.

Even in Job's trials, he has joy in one thing: he rejoiced that he had not denied the words of the Holy One. This was no mean feat. His wife had advised him earlier, "Do you still hold fast your integrity? Curse God and die!"

Job's answer is well known: "You speak as one of the foolish women speaks. Shall we indeed accept good from God and not accept adversity?"

In chapter 6, Job is not just *passively accepting* his afflictions; he is *rejoicing* that he has not denied God in them. He rejoices that, while experiencing awful pain, he knows he has still not sinned against the Holy One. We, too, can rejoice when we have victory over the temptation to sin.

If afflictions were a good cause to deny God, Job would have had ample reasons for disregarding His Word. We line up our excuses ahead of time. When we get angry over something, we are ready with excuses such as not enough sleep, a hard day, lots of things going wrong at work or in the home. There are no excuses for sin. But obedience is always possible, and we can rejoice when that is the choice we make.

Job did not rejoice in his adversity because everything was going to turn out rosy. As far as he knew, no such outcome was on the horizon. Job rejoiced in his obedience, as can we.

DAY

97

Sacrifice for Others

For we rejoice when we ourselves are weak but you are strong; this we also pray for, that you be made complete. (2 Cor. 13:9)

Paul suffered a lot for the Corinthians. He wanted them to be strong. If that meant that he and others with him in ministry were weakened, so be it. His joy was in seeing them flourish. He gave no thought to the cost to himself.

Good parents have this attitude in regards to their children. They may not care what sacrifices they make for their children to be successful. Paul has that same view towards the believers in Corinth. Like a parent who is responsible to save up for his children, he put it all out there, willingly, joyfully (2 Cor. 12:14).

Paul was serving the church, and we should do the same. This is not to say you have to be the Sunday school coordinator. But you should be working so that the body of believers flourishes. Then when you see the church flourishing, even if you sacrificed a lot to accomplish it, you can rejoice.

Hold Them in High Regard

Therefore I have sent him all the more eagerly so that when you see him again you may rejoice and I may be less concerned about you. Receive him then in the Lord with all joy, and hold men like him in high regard; because he came close to death for the work of Christ, risking his life to complete what was deficient in your service to me. (Phil. 2:28–30)

Philippians is known as the epistle of joy because it is a prominent theme. Suffering is also a theme in the letter (1:7, 13–14, 21, 28–29; 2:8, 17, 27–30; 3:8, 10; 4:12–14).

Epaphroditus had been sent to Paul with a gift and then became ill in Rome, apparently as a result of that trip. Paul says that he was sick "to the point of death." But he was eager to return to Philippi, and Paul was eager to send him so that the Philippians could rejoice.

Paul tells them to not only receive Epaphroditus with joy, but also to hold men such as him in high regard. His brush with death was due to the work of Christ (v. 30).

"Sending churches" can get complacent after sending money to their missionaries overseas. It is sometimes difficult to feel how much such help means to those who are far away. We can be a bit out of sight, out of mind. When your emissary returns and has suffered physically as a result of their work, if you are a bit nonchalant about it, you need to be reminded to receive them in the Lord with joy—real joy because it is in the Lord, not fake joy because you have to.

Joy and Crown

For our citizenship is in heaven, from which also we eagerly wait for a Savior, the Lord Jesus Christ; who will transform the body of our humble state into conformity with the body of His glory, by the exertion of the power that He has even to subject all things to Himself. Therefore, *my beloved brethren whom I long to see, my joy and crown,* in this way stand firm in the Lord, my beloved. (Phil. 3:20–4:1)

This section comes hot on the heels of Paul's description of those "whose end is destruction" and "who set their minds on earthly things" (v. 19). In contrast, he says that the Philippians are his joy and crown, and their citizenship is in heaven. Paul goes on to explain how different this citizenship is. We wait "eagerly for a Savior, the Lord Jesus Christ" (v. 20). And this is no small thing, for "He will transform the body of our humble state into conformity with the body of His glory" (v. 20). How different this is from those whose god is their appetite, and whose glory is in their shame!

Chapter 4 starts out with the word *therefore.* "Therefore . . .in this way stand firm in the Lord" (v. 1). In what way? By realizing where our citizenship is.

When he writes about our Lord Jesus Christ, Paul always expands on the primary thought. In 3:20, he doesn't just say, "We eagerly wait for a Savior, the Lord Jesus Christ," and stop there. He immediately follows it up with how Jesus will transform us from our humble state into conformity with the body of His glory, etc., etc.

As Paul writes this, I see his eagerness to relate this wonderful state of things to the Philippians, who are his joy and crown. He is not just sending this to unknown believers; they are dear to him, they are his joy.

Rejoicing Before God

For what thanks can we render to God for you in return for all the joy with which we rejoice before our God on your account, as we night and day keep praying most earnestly that we may see your face, and may complete what is lacking in your faith? (1 Thess. 3:9–10)

Paul is not able to thank God enough for all the joy he has because of the Thessalonians. Paul & Co. had been worried about the Thessalonians, so they sent Timothy to strengthen and encourage them. Paul's fear was that the tempter would have tempted them and as a result, all of Paul's (et al.) labor would have been for nothing.

Then Timothy came back with a report of their solid faith and love, which resulted in Paul's expression, "For now, we really live, if you stand firm in the Lord" (v. 8). This report brought about the feeling that they could not thank God enough.

But notice where their joy was: "for all the joy with which we rejoice before our God, on your account." They were rejoicing because of the good news about the Thessalonians, but they were rejoicing *before God*. When we have something to rejoice about, that joy should be "before our God." He is the one that gives us joy.

Rejoicing in the Body

And if one member suffers, all the members suffer with it; if one member is honored, all the members rejoice with it. (1 Cor. 12:26)

1 Corinthians 12 teaches on the body of Christ, the church. No part of the body is more important than another. Every one has his or her own function. We need to recognize this and act on it. There should be no jealousy; on the contrary, there should be joy when one part of the body is honored.

This is real joy in others. There is no room for, "I wish that were me!" We know that a hand is not a foot, nor an ear an eye, but maybe, just maybe, I want to be honored like an eye, even if I am an appendix. I don't want to *be* an eye; I just want everyone to recognize my contribution like theirs is recognized.

No. *They are honored, I rejoice.* And I, like the appendix, should not be the only one rejoicing. The whole body is to rejoice—the big toe, the salivary glands, every part. This is because the different parts of the body perform their duties "for the common good" (v. 7).

What can we take away from this very useful metaphor? We may have a pastor that is asked to speak at a national conference. Many in the congregation will rejoice, but maybe the assistant pastor thinks he could have done a better job. His joy is tepid.

Joy for other parts of the body of Christ being honored does not allow for jealousy in any shape or form. This kind of jealousy is often downplayed as not being unhappy for the one honored, but wanting that honor, too. "Yes, I *am* happy for them, but I want it, too." This really douses the actual joy you have for your brother or sister in Christ. Your eyes are focused on *yourself*, and they are just in your peripheral vision.

Rejoice in others being honored!

SECTION ELEVEN

Rejoicing for Things

God at Work

The crowds with one accord were giving attention to what was said by Philip, as they heard and saw the signs which he was performing. For in the case of many who had unclean spirits, they were coming out of them shouting with a loud voice; and many who had been paralyzed and lame were healed. So there was much rejoicing in that city. (Acts 8:6–8)

Here the city rejoices in the healing of the paralyzed and lame as well as those possessed by unclean spirits. The rejoicing in the city is contrasted with the unclean spirits, who didn't seem to be doing the same. They were coming out shouting with a loud voice.

When we hear of someone being surprisingly healed, we rejoice (although some of us are dubious). When we see God answering our prayers, we also rejoice. The rejoicing all boils down to *seeing God at work* in our immediate sphere.

All Who Seek You

Let all who seek You rejoice
and be glad in You;
Let those who love Your
salvation say continually,
"The LORD be magnified!"
(Psalm 40:16)

Those who seek God rejoice. Seeking Him leads to salvation, and the natural response to salvation is to praise the LORD. We magnify the LORD for our salvation, and because we have sought Him, joy is the fruit. This is followed by continual praise for that salvation.

The Joy of Fellowship

Since I have had for many years a longing to come to you whenever I go to Spain—for I hope to see you in passing, and to be helped on my way there by you, when I have first enjoyed your company for awhile . . . . Now I urge you, brethren, by our Lord Jesus Christ and by the love of the Spirit, to strive together with me in your prayers to God for me, that I may be rescued from those who are disobedient in Judea, and that my service for Jerusalem may prove acceptable to the saints; so that I may come to you in joy by the will of God, and find refreshing rest in your company. (Rom. 15:23, 30–32)

Paul planned to travel to Spain, but he had to go to Jerusalem first to deliver a gift. On his way back, heading for Spain, he would stop by Rome to rejoice in fellowship with the believers there and be refreshingly rested in their company. This trip seems to have been contingent on his service to the saints in Jerusalem being acceptable to them. He asks for the believers in Rome to "strive together with him in their prayers to God" for him. He wanted their help through prayers.

Joy in fellowship was something that Paul expected and counted on. This type of joy is often disparaged because it is in someone other than God. After a church retreat, people refer to the resultant joy as something that won't last, a *high*, as if it were a drug. But God has given us other believers to have joy in. Paul was looking forward to enjoying the Roman belivers' fellowship.

However, it must be noted that joy in the fellowship of other believers requires that they actually *are* believers. It also requires there to be no unforgiving hearts between them, no bitterness, and no other unconfessed sin that would hinder fellowship.

Joy in Receiving Gifts

I rejoice over the coming of Stephanas and Fortunatus and Achaicus, because they have supplied what was lacking on your part. For they have refreshed my spirit and yours. Therefore acknowledge such men. (1 Cor. 16:17–18)

These three men made Paul happy because they brought support from the Corinthian church. Their presence itself was also refreshing to Paul's spirit. They had done the same refreshing for the Corinthian church. These men had done a service for both Paul and the Corinthians, and what they did was rightly acknowledged.

There is joy in fellowship and in receiving gifts (although you might think the second sounds unspiritual). There is also a benefit to the giver, especially when the gift meets a need. "Not that I seek the gift itself, but I seek the profit which increases to your account. But I have received everything in full and have an abundance; I am amply supplied, having received from Epaphroditus what you have sent, a fragrant aroma, an acceptable sacrifice, well-pleasing to God" (Phil. 4:17–18). In this passage, we see that giving also blesses those who give; the gift was a profit to their account. In this case, Paul was thankful; in the Corinthian passage, the gift gave him joy.

There is nothing unspiritual in rejoicing as a result of gifts. There is only a problem if there is a critical spirit, the very opposite of joy and thanksgiving.

Faithful Are the Wounds of a Friend

This is the very thing I wrote you so that when I came, I would not have sorrow from those who ought to make me rejoice, having confidence in you that my joy would be the joy of you all. For out of much affliction and anguish of heart I wrote to you with many tears; not so that you would be made sorrowful, but that you might know the love which I have especially for you. (2 Cor. 2:3–4)

At the beginning of chapter 2, Paul said he was determined to not come to the Corinthians in sorrow again. In 1 Corinthians 5, he had corrected them for tolerating sin in their midst, and they were sorrowful about it.
There is a proverb that speaks of this very problem:

> Better is open rebuke
> Than love that is concealed.

> Faithful are the wounds of a friend,
> But deceitful are the kisses of an enemy.
> (Proverbs 27:5–6)

Paul was a faithful friend to the Corinthians and therefore rebuked them. But he wasn't still angry with them, especially since they had taken care of the problem.

DAY

107

The Joy of Repentance

But God, who comforts the depressed, comforted us by the coming of Titus; and not only by his coming, but also by the comfort with which he was comforted in you, as he reported to us your longing, your mourning, your zeal for me; so that I rejoiced even more. For though I caused you sorrow by my letter, I do not regret it; though I did regret it—for I see that that letter caused you sorrow, though only for a while—*I now rejoice, not that you were made sorrowful, but that you were made sorrowful to the point of repentance;* for you were made sorrowful according to the will of God, so that you might not suffer loss in anything through us. For the sorrow that is according to the will of God produces a repentance without regret, leading to salvation, but the sorrow of the world produces death. For behold what earnestness this very thing, this godly sorrow, has produced in you: what vindication of yourselves, what indignation, what fear, what longing, what zeal, what avenging of wrong! In everything, you demonstrated yourselves to be innocent in the matter. So although I wrote to you, it was not for the sake of the offender nor for the sake of the one offended, but that your earnestness on our behalf might be made known to you in the sight of God. For this reason, we have been comforted. And besides our comfort, we rejoiced even much more for the joy of Titus, because his spirit has been refreshed by you all. (2 Cor. 6:7–13)

This passage speaks to the joy of fellowship in good and bad situations. There are three things that Paul is rejoicing about in this passage:

- The Corinthians longed for Paul, mourned for him, and had a zeal for God. We can understand why they longed for Paul. He was away from them, and they had messed up. Their zeal for him could be connected to his bringing the gospel to them initially. Their mourning is perhaps referring to their repentance and their sorrow that they had disappointed him. These three things indicated to Paul how the Corinthians viewed him, and that brought him even more joy.
- The Corinthians were sorrowful to the point of repentance. Paul was not a masochist; he was sad that he needed to write a letter that would make

them sad—but he didn't regret it. It was necessary, but his joy came in their repentance, which he learned of from Titus.

- Titus was joyful due to his visit to Corinth and his being refreshed by the believers there. Paul say that he had joy because of Titus' joy. This brings to mind Romans 12:15: "Rejoice with those who rejoice, and weep with those who weep."

Truth Applied

I rejoice that in everything I have confidence in you. (2 Cor. 7:16)

There has been correction from Paul, then encouragement and thanksgiving for the Corinthian believers. Now Paul is encouraging the Corinthians with his statement of confidence. It is not generic confidence; he is confident that he can rejoice that they will follow his teaching in everything.

It is a great feeling for a teacher when what they teach is learned and learned well and the students are sure to apply their knowledge in the right place and at the right time. Teachers can rejoice in this.

How much more a minister of the gospel with the followers of Christ! For a faithful preacher, it is a joyful thing when those whom he ministers to both learn and apply what they have heard from the pulpit.

Face to Face

Though I have many things to write to you, I do not want to do so with paper and ink; but I hope to come to you and speak face to face, so that your joy may be made full. (2 John 12)

John kept his letter short because he wanted to speak to them face to face. Why? So that their joy would be made full.

There is joy in being together with other believers. There is joy in seeing one another after a time of separation. A letter or a phone call from a loved one far away will bring joy—even more so seeing one another over a video chat. But nothing beats being in each other's presence.

Just think of those video clips of a dad coming home from a tour of duty overseas and showing up at his kid's school as a surprise. The joy is to the point of tears. After that, there is speaking face to face, speaking of all that has happened in the intervening time.

John has so much to say to them that he doesn't want to write it. He will go see them, and they all will have full joy.

Encouragement

So when they were sent away, they went down to Antioch; and having gathered the congregation together they delivered the letter. When they had read it, they rejoiced because of its encouragement. (Acts 15:30–31)

You just know there is a story behind this letter. The rest of Acts 15 gives the context: some men had come to the church in Antioch and started teaching that the Gentiles needed to be circumcised.

An intense debate followed, at the end of which Peter stood up to say that there was no difference between Jews and Gentiles when it came to salvation, since both had their hearts cleansed by faith (v. 9). Then he wraps it up with these words: "But we believe that we are saved through the grace of the Lord Jesus, in the same way as they also are" (v. 11).

After the issue was settled in Jerusalem, James wrote a letter to the Gentile believers in Antioch, Syria, and Cilicia telling them that there was no need to become Jews in order to be saved. They only needed to "abstain from things contaminated by idols, from fornication and from what is strangled and from blood" (v. 20).

This whole issue had caused great concern among the Gentile believers, and they were waiting for the reply. When they read the letter, they rejoiced because of its encouragement.

Encouragement is a cause for joy. We can respond to it with joy. We can also give others joy by encouraging them. In this particular case, it is encouragement in the right doctrine, but that is not the only subject on which we can encourage the brethren.

Rejoicing in Obedience

Now I urge you, brethren, keep your eye on those who cause dissensions and hindrances contrary to the teaching which you learned, and turn away from them. For such men are slaves, not of our Lord Christ but of their own appetites; and by their smooth and flattering speech, they deceive the hearts of the unsuspecting. For the report of your obedience has reached to all; therefore I am rejoicing over you, but I want you to be wise in what is good and innocent in what is evil. (Rom. 16:17–19)

Here there is a warning and an encouragement. Certain teachers were causing disagreements and hindrances among the believers in Rome. Paul told the believers to turn away from such men. The believers didn't have to worry about hurting their feelings, for they were deceivers, slaves of their own appetite. They were after unsuspecting people, which the Romans Christians were.

But Paul was encouraged by the Roman believers *because their obedience was well known*, and he was rejoicing over them. Paul is once again affirming the joy he had in them.

We can also have joy in our fellow believers. This does not preclude teaching them and encouraging them to greater obedience. Rejoice in someone's obedience doesn't require them to be perfect. Sometimes we think that we can have joy in someone else only if they are as close to perfect as we think possible. It is wonderful when a little kid learns his letters. The parents should rejoice in this at the same time as they realize that there is so much more ahead. The fact that these believers had been taught and taught well did not mean there was nothing more to learn.

The men Paul warned the Roman believers about were trying to lead them astray. So right after he tells them that he is rejoicing over them, Paul encourages them to be wise in good and innocent of evil. When you are wise in the good, the evil becomes obvious.

Again, Paul rejoices in these people not because they were above it all or had learned everything, but because of their obedience to what they did know.

Answered Prayer

I rejoice over the coming of Stephanas and Fortunatus and Achaicus, because they have supplied what was lacking on your part. For they have refreshed my spirit and yours. Therefore acknowledge such men. (1 Cor. 16:17–18)

These three men brought something from the Corinthians that they had promised and that Paul was in need of. He rejoiced when they showed up with that supply. What they brought was refreshing to all concerned.

But where does the joy fit in here?

- They brought what was both needed and promised, which was an answer to prayer.
- Because of their coming, Paul was refreshed, which also refreshed the Corinthians.
- The passage implies that the joy was not entirely in the gift itself but because the gift showed how the Corinthians viewed Paul.

Even when we really believe we will receive an answer, answered prayer still gives great joy. This was the case in Acts 12 when Peter was released from jail—first astonishment that God had answered their prayers, then great joy.

DAY

113

Of the Same Mind

Therefore if there is any encouragement in Christ, if there is any consolation of love, if there is any fellowship of the Spirit, if any affection and compassion, *make my joy complete* by being of the same mind, maintaining the same love, united in spirit, intent on one purpose. (Phil. 2:1–2)

Here is a fine example of rhetorical statements, i.e., when the response is obvious. "Can fish swim?" "Is the pope Catholic?"

"If there is any encouragement in Christ . . ." Well, of course there is!

"If there is any consolation of love . . ." Of course there is!

"If there is any fellowship of the Spirit . . ." Yes, of course there is!

"If there is any affection and compassion . . ." You guessed it. There is!

If the reply to all these *if* statements is, "Of course there is," then what are the Philippians to do? They are *to make Paul's joy complete* by 1) being of the same mind, 2) maintaining the same love, 3) being united in spirit and 4) intent on one purpose.

This is what you could call a common problem to all believers everywhere. This is a *command* to us, not a wish list or a timely suggestion. *If* the statements above are true (and we know they are), then this unity is required.

The passage doesn't stop with this. "Do nothing from selfishness or empty conceit, but with humility consider one another as more important than yourselves; do not merely look out for your own personal interests, but also for the interests of others" (vv. 3–4). We are told to do nothing from selfishness and to regard others as more important than ourselves.

In fact, we are to have the same attitude as Christ Jesus did when He left heaven to come and die for us. "Have this attitude in yourselves which was also in Christ Jesus, who, as He already existed in the form of God, did not consider equality with God something to be grasped, but emptied Himself by taking the form of a bondservant and being born in the likeness of men. And being found in appearance as a man, He humbled Himself by becoming obedient to the point of death: death on a cross" (vv. 5–8).

This is where all the Christians say in unison, "But we are only human!" Go back to verse 1. We agreed that there is encouragement in Christ, fellowship of the Spirit, etc. Therefore, we might be unwilling to obey verse 2, but *we are able* to obey it.

Many of us (or all of us, really) would be more than willing to be of the same mind, as long as it was *our* mind, not another's. What is particularly sad about this is that many of us would not rejoice, as Paul says he would, if all the Christians we knew were of the same mind.

This unity of mind is attached to verses 5–11, which are all about Christ emptying Himself, humbling Himself, dying for us, and then being exalted above every name. In the end, we will all bow our knees and confess that Jesus Christ is Lord, to God's glory!

This is the encouragement of Christ; this is the consolation of love; this is the fellowship of the Spirit. All Christians, if they are Christians, have already bowed their knees to Christ and His Father. Because of that, we can be of the same mind, we can maintain the same love, and we can be united in spirit and intent on one purpose.

What joy would follow from our leaders! Well, maybe not so much if they are intent on being "more right" on secondary or tertiary doctrines. Humans take pleasure in being right. If we all are busy focusing on our union in Christ (even if we still disagree on secondary doctrines), no one gets to be the one who's right! But Paul would have been joyful, and we know that unity of the believers is what Jesus prayed for (John 17:22–23).

For more on this subject, I recommend reading *I Have Given Them the Glory* by my father, Jim Wilson.[2]

2. Available on Amazon and at ccmbooks.org.

His Lovingkindness

I will rejoice and be glad in Your lovingkindness,
Because You have seen my affliction;
You have known the troubles of my soul,
And You have not given me over into the hand of the enemy;
You have set my feet in a large place.
(Psalm 31:7–8)

As believers, we understand this truth from the very beginning of our Christian life. When we are forgiven, we know what mercy, what lovingkindness, God extended to us. The more we understand this (growing in this knowledge is lifelong), the more we will rejoice in it.

Our joy hinges on God's mercy, of which there is no end. "It is of the LORD's mercies that we are not consumed, because his compassions fail not. They are new every morning: great is thy faithfulness" (Lam. 3:22–23).

DAY

115

Rejoicing in His Blessings

You shall not act like this toward the LORD your God. But you shall seek the LORD at the place which the LORD your God will choose from all your tribes, to establish His name there for His dwelling, and there you shall come. There you shall bring your burnt offerings, your sacrifices, your tithes, the contribution of your hand, your votive offerings, your freewill offerings, and the firstborn of your herd and of your flock. There also you and your households shall eat before the LORD your God and rejoice in all your undertakings in which the LORD your God has blessed you . . . . And you shall rejoice before the LORD your God, you and your sons and daughters, your male and female servants, and the Levite who is within your gates, since he has no portion or inheritance with you . . . . But you shall eat them before the LORD your God in the place which the LORD your God will choose, you and your son and daughter, and your male and female servants, and the Levite who is within your gates; and you shall rejoice before the LORD your God in all your undertakings. (Deut. 12:4–7, 12, 18)

You may spend the money for whatever your heart desires: for oxen, or sheep, or wine, or strong drink, or whatever your heart desires; and there you shall eat in the presence of the Lord your God and rejoice, you and your household. (Deut. 14:26)

God is telling His people what to do when they enter the Promised Land. In Deuteronomy 12:1–3, He tells them to "utterly destroy" all the worship places of the pagan people, obliterating the names of their gods. There was to be no overlap or whitewashing of paganism.

The site of the future temple had not been determined, but sacrifices and offerings were made at the tabernacle. But worship at the tabernacle (and later the temple) was not just about sacrifices. Following the sacrifices and offerings, the families were to *rejoice*. The rejoicing was to be specifically in regard to all the things in which the LORD had blessed them. The banquet was a joyful time together recognizing the LORD's blessings on them.

Some Christians ask why we feast at holidays (Easter, Thanksgiving, Christmas) when our joy is about God and what He has done, not about us. We are celebrating His birth, but we give gifts to *each other*? What's that about?

In this passage, *God tells us to feast* because of His care for us, because of what He has done for us. That specifically applies to all the holidays mentioned above. God sent His Son as a baby who would grow up and die for us. Let us banquet because He has done this. He has provided food and plenty. Let's feast and thank Him.

In Deuteronomy 12:12, the people of Israel are told to sacrifice and give offerings, and after that everybody was to rejoice before the Lord their God. That included even the servants. When we think of *sacrifice*, we think of giving up what we don't want to give up. We view it as a duty, not a joy. But in Deuteronomy, sacrifices to the Lord and joy before the Lord are closely connected.

We are to rejoice before the Lord about the blessings He has bestowed on us. And He has bestowed *many* of those.

DAY

116

Celebrating Thanksgiving

"Now behold, I have brought the first of the produce of the ground which You, O LORD, have given me." And you shall set it down before the LORD your God, and worship before the LORD your God; and you and the Levite and the alien who is among you shall rejoice in all the good which the LORD your God has given you and your household. (Deut. 26:10–11)

The Israelites make an offering to the LORD at the beginning of harvest. After the offering and worship before Him, the people (including the clergy and the foreigners) are to rejoice "in all the good which the LORD our God has given us and our households." This is very like the American custom of Thanksgiving. We are blessed, and we thank God; we also rejoice in His blessings.

There is no guilt in this prosperity at all. If God has prospered us, we give Him the firstfruits, and we share it with everybody, including the clergy and foreigners.

A Wise Son

When Hiram heard the words of Solomon, he rejoiced greatly and said, "Blessed be the LORD today, who has given to David a wise son over this great people." (1 Kings 5:7)

Hiram was the king of Tyre, hired by King Solomon to supply materials for the temple in Jerusalem. It was a big contract, and Hiram recognized that. How does he respond to the news? First, he *rejoiced greatly.* This seems to simply mean he rejoices in the good that has come to him, the prosperity that he and his kingdom will enjoy. He then blesses the LORD for giving King David such a wise son in Solomon. Hiram's rejoicing is connected with the LORD and His blessing David through this wise son, which blessed Hiram in prospering him.

Joy recognizes God's hand in our blessings.

The Way of Your Testimonies

I have rejoiced in the way of Your testimonies,
As much as in all riches.
(Psalm 119:14)

Here is a comparison of two different reasons for rejoicing. Because riches are tangible, it is relatively easy to rejoice in them, even in a godly way, thanking the LORD for them. It's all good. The author of Psalm 119 rejoices in God's testimonies (the law, precepts, statutes, and commandments of God). It is interesting that the composer of this psalm could rejoice in the abstract law, but also in the concrete "way of His testimonies." This is *joy in obedience*, walking in the way of God's word.

The Wealth of the Nations

Arise, shine; for your light has come,
And the glory of the Lord has risen upon you.
For behold, darkness will cover the earth
And deep darkness the peoples;
But the Lord will rise upon you
And His glory will appear upon you.
Nations will come to your light,
And kings to the brightness of your rising.
Lift up your eyes round about and see;
They all gather together, they come to you.
Your sons will come from afar,
And your daughters will be carried on the hip.
Then you will see and be radiant,
And your heart will thrill and rejoice
Because the abundance of the sea will be turned to you,
The wealth of the nations will come to you.
(Isa. 60:1–5)

In 1776, Adam Smith used a phrase from verse 5—*The Wealth of Nations*—as the title of a treatise that ushered in the new age of capitalism. However, that is not the subject here.

This passage is talking about prosperity as a result of the LORD's glory shining upon His people. Verses 1–3 show that it is talking about a specific time.

The glory of the LORD is a key element in the subsequent events: nations coming to Israel's light, kings also coming to their brightness. Why? Because the glory of the LORD has risen upon them. The rest of the chapter continues in the same vein.

It is clear from the context that this is not a run-of-the-mill good economic time. It is a prophecy of a time when the church shall reign. It is described, however, in economic terms.

The God of All Comfort

"For the LORD has ransomed Jacob
And redeemed him from the hand of him who was stronger than he.
They will come and shout for joy on the height of Zion,
And they will be radiant over the bounty of the LORD—
Over the grain and the new wine and the oil,
And over the young of the flock and the herd;
And their life will be like a watered garden,
And they will never languish again.
Then the virgin will rejoice in the dance,
And the young men and the old, together,
For I will turn their mourning into joy
And will comfort them and give them joy for their sorrow.
I will fill the soul of the priests with abundance,
And My people will be satisfied with My goodness,"
Declares the LORD.
(Jer. 31:11–14)

Jeremiah has just spent twenty-nine chapters prophesying the captivity of Judah. But the future is not all doom and gloom. Deliverance is promised. They will not always be slaves to a foreign kingdom. "But they shall serve the LORD their God and David their King, whom I will raise up for them" (30:9).

Whenever the fortunes of Judah are good, it is connected to their obedience to the LORD. Here Jeremiah prophesies that they will be redeemed from captivity and will "come and shout for joy on the height of Zion." Then God will give them physical blessings—grain, new wine, oil, the young of the flock and herd.

How are the people rejoicing? They are dancing—all of them, from the virgins to the old men. God promises to comfort them and replace their sorrow with joy. God's comfort is the first cause of joy, then the physical blessings.

SCRIPTURE INDEX